I0020933

Instant SASS CSS How-to

Learn to write more efficient CSS with the help of the SASS CSS library using practical, hands-on recipes

Alex Libby

PUBLISHING

BIRMINGHAM - MUMBAI

Instant SASS CSS How-to

Copyright © 2013 Packt Publishing

All rights reserved. No part of this book may be reproduced, stored in a retrieval system, or transmitted in any form or by any means, without the prior written permission of the publisher, except in the case of brief quotations embedded in critical articles or reviews.

Every effort has been made in the preparation of this book to ensure the accuracy of the information presented. However, the information contained in this book is sold without warranty, either express or implied. Neither the author, nor Packt Publishing, and its dealers and distributors will be held liable for any damages caused or alleged to be caused directly or indirectly by this book.

Packt Publishing has endeavored to provide trademark information about all of the companies and products mentioned in this book by the appropriate use of capitals. However, Packt Publishing cannot guarantee the accuracy of this information.

First published: February 2013

Production Reference: 1180213

Published by Packt Publishing Ltd.
Livery Place
35 Livery Street
Birmingham B3 2PB, UK.

ISBN 978-1-78216-378-7

www.packtpub.com

Credits

Author
Alex Libby

Reviewer
Melanie Archer

Acquisition Editor
Kartikey Pandey

Commissioning Editor
Maria D'souza

Technical Editor
Veronica Fernandes

Project Coordinator
Esha Thakker

Proofreader
Lindsey Thomas

Production Coordinator
Melwyn D'sa

Cover Work
Melwyn D'sa

Cover Image
Sheetal Aute

About the Author

Alex Libby has background in IT support – he has been involved in supporting end users for the last 15 years in a variety of different environments, and currently works as a technical analyst, supporting a medium-sized SharePoint estate for an international parts distributor based in the UK. Although he gets to play with different technologies in his day job, his first true love has always been with the open source movement, and in particular experimenting with CSS/CSS3 and HTML5. To date, Alex has written two books (one on HTML5 video and another on JQuery tools) – *Instant SASS CSS How-to* is his third book.

I'd like to thank my family and friends for their help and encouragement, Maria D'souza for her help and guidance in writing the book, and Melanie for providing lots of constructive comments with the reviewing – without them, I am sure I wouldn't have been able to produce this book!

About the Reviewer

Melanie Archer is a web developer living in Oakland, California, USA. Since hand-coding her first web page in 1997, she's worked with many corporations, design agencies, and startups to bring standards-compliant delight to dozens of user interfaces. Other titles she has reviewed include *HTML5 Boilerplate Web Development, Divya Manian, Packt Publishing*.

You can follow Melanie on Twitter at `@mejarc`.

www.PacktPub.com

Support files, eBooks, discount offers and more

You might want to visit www.PacktPub.com for support files and downloads related to your book.

Did you know that Packt offers eBook versions of every book published, with PDF and ePub files available? You can upgrade to the eBook version at www.PacktPub.com and as a print book customer, you are entitled to a discount on the eBook copy. Get in touch with us at service@packtpub.com for more details.

At www.PacktPub.com, you can also read a collection of free technical articles, sign up for a range of free newsletters and receive exclusive discounts and offers on Packt books and eBooks.

http://PacktLib.PacktPub.com

Do you need instant solutions to your IT questions? PacktLib is Packt's online digital book library. Here, you can access, read and search across Packt's entire library of books.

Why Subscribe?

- ► Fully searchable across every book published by Packt
- ► Copy and paste, print and bookmark content
- ► On demand and accessible via web browser

Free Access for Packt account holders

If you have an account with Packt at www.PacktPub.com, you can use this to access PacktLib today and view nine entirely free books. Simply use your login credentials for immediate access.

Table of Contents

Preface

Imagine the following scenario:

You're an accomplished developer, working on a high profile project for a demanding client. You're normally a fairly patient kind of person, but even this client is proving a little bit too much of a challenge...when you get that phone call you dread.

"Alex...you know those buttons you kindly changed for me last week? I'm really sorry, but could we please try a different color, as the boss really doesn't like that shade of red!"

This is where you silently curse – that's more than 60 buttons, littered with browser-specific CSS prefixes; a real pain in the neck, which you could well do without, particularly as it took you a couple of hours to make the changes last time. (Yes, it's a big site, before you ask!). Sounds familiar? Wish there was another way to do this? I thought so – welcome to the world of SASS!

SASS, I hear you ask? What's this all about then? Well, I could give you the technical low-down, but it's probably better demonstrated by the use of an example. Do you remember those 60 buttons I mentioned earlier? What if you could change the color of all of those buttons in one go? Yes, you read right, all of those buttons. This is just a small part of what SASS can achieve, as a superset of CSS3. We can use the power of SASS to set a variable that you could use to change the color value set against all buttons in one go, with a single click.

Intrigued? We will look at this and more throughout this book, so let's make a start...

What this book covers

Throughout this book, we're going to look at a variety of exercises that are designed to help you become accustomed to working with the basics of the LESS CSS preprocessor language. You're probably wondering what we're going to cover, right? No problem – let me reveal all:

Downloading and installing SASS (Must know) is the most important part of this book – here, we take a look at how to download and install SASS. Depending on which platform you prefer to use, it can be really easy, or somewhat more involved.

Adding support to text editors (Must know) will take you through how to add support for SASS to your favorite text editor. In this recipe, we'll use Sublime Text 2 as our editor, but the principles could equally apply to other editors that you may prefer to use.

Pre-compiling SASS (Must know) will show you that you don't always have to rely on the command line to compile SASS; there are alternatives available that can do the heavy work for you. In this recipe, I'll show you how, using Scout. We'll also look at a means to convert CSS back to SCSS, although it is not without its shortcomings

Viewing SASS in a browser (Become an expert) is crucial to help debug any style issues in your code. There will be moments when you've written a style, only to find it's not working as you expected. No problem – I'll show you some ways to view this information, depending on which browser you prefer to use.

Using nested rules (Must know) in SASS is a good way to reduce repetition in your code. In this recipe, we'll start our coding journey by looking at how you can use SASS to nest your CSS rules, to avoid such repetition.

Using comments in SASS (Should know) will probably be one of the most important things you use in SASS when starting out. After all we're only human, and you won't be able to remember what each style is meant to do, once you complete your project! In this recipe we'll see how to add comments in this task, and when to use the different types available.

Getting interactive with Script (Become an expert) may at first appear easy, but it's simplicity belies its true power. In this recipe, you'll learn how you can easily check the results of any mathematical formula you decide to use in writing SASS. Not sure what I mean? Here's why you'll see margin-left: 5px + 8px/2px equals 9px, and not 6.5px, as you might otherwise expect.

Using CSS-3 directives in SASS (Must know) will be a lifesaver, particularly for anyone who uses responsive design techniques. You are very likely to have used keywords such as @media or @import in your code, but have you nested your CSS-3 directives before? In this recipe, I'll show you how you can achieve this and more, using SASS.

Controlling output in SASS (Must know) will show you how you can really save time when working with lots of repeating styles. In this recipe, you'll see how you can use the power of SASS to dynamically create styles for multiple items that use the same styles, such as a group of social media buttons.

Creating and using mixins (Must know) is probably one of the most frequent things you will do when working with SASS. In this recipe, we'll see how you can start to build your own mixins, that you can easily reuse in your projects. We'll also see how you can start to reduce (or even avoid) duplication of styles that you might otherwise have in your projects.

Building functions within SASS (Must know) is no different to using functions in other programming languages. In this recipe, you'll see how you can use the power of SASS to dynamically create styles in CSS, using functions to work out the appropriate style, based on the values you use.

Altering output style (Should know) of your CSS will make you wish you had started using CSS a long time ago. SASS has the ability to use a number of different styles when producing your style sheet output, and maintains a consistent format when using SASS. In this recipe, we'll take a look at the styles available, and how to enable them in your code.

Using a pre-built mixin library (Should know) when working in SASS may seem like a shortcut, but I'm a great believer in "why reinvent the wheel?". We've talked about writing our own mixins throughout this book. It is worth looking online though, to see if people have already created a suitable library available for your needs. In this recipe, we'll take a look at one such example, available from `lesselements.com`.

Writing mixins – developing a style (Must know) will show you how it can be advantageous to develop your own style when writing mixins in your projects. This recipe will give you some tips you can use, to help in developing your own style when writing mixins, functions, and so on, when developing in SASS.

Downloading and installing Compass (Should know) will take a look at another, well-known library that is often used by developers using SASS, that contains a whole host of useful mixins that you can use. In this recipe, we'll learn how to download and install the library on your own system, ready for use.

Creating sprites using Compass and SASS (Become an expert) will show you how easy it is to produce sprites. You'll soon be on the way to producing them with little fuss, although there are a few gotchas you'll need to be aware of.

Using vendor prefixes and Compass (Become an expert) takes you through how you can avoid the necessary evil that is the bane of every developer's life: vendor prefixes. Fortunately though, Compass makes this really easy. In this recipe, we'll see how, through the use of mixins, vendor prefix issues will become a thing of the past

Building a slider using Compass (Become an expert) takes you through how you can apply some of the skills we've covered, and puts them to good use building a content slider. In this recipe, you'll see how we can use the power of WooTheme's FlexSlider library, and a little help from SASS and Compass, to produce something you can drop in to your future projects, or use as a starting point for further development

Using SASS with WordPress (Become an expert) will take you through how you can begin to apply some of the techniques we've looked at throughout this book, within the confines of a CMS system. In this recipe (and the next), we'll take a look at how you can use it in WordPress. Although the same principles will apply to most (if not all) CMS systems.

Using Compass in WordPress (Become an expert) is where we can really show off the power of SASS and Compass. In this recipe, we'll use the same principles as before, but with Compass. I'll show you how you can begin to adapt a theme to use SASS, and make your development work a lot easier.

What you need for this book

There will be instances where you may need to install software for a particular recipe – we will go through the specifics of each piece of software, ahead of any task. In the meantime, you will need the following:

> ► An internet connection – for downloading various pieces of software for each recipe.
>
> ► A working installation of WordPress – for the form demo towards the end of the book.
>
> ► A modern browser – it must be one capable of running CSS3. Ideal examples would be the latest versions of Firefox, Safari, Chrome, or IE. We will look at backward compatibility in older browsers, but the effect will not be the same.
>
> ► A text editor – there are hundreds available for free or at a low cost. Alternatively, you can use something like Notepad. My personal preference is Textpad, a shareware application which is available at `http://www.textpad.com`.

Who this book is for

This book is great for those who may or may not already manage a website of some description, but want to learn how CSS pre-processing can help with streamlining their development workflow, and help reduce the amount of code they need to write. You may or may not already have some familiarity with Ruby.

Conventions

In this book, you will find a number of styles of text that distinguish between different kinds of information. Here are some examples of these styles, and an explanation of their meaning.

Code words in text are shown as follows: "We can include other contexts through the use of the `include` directive."

A block of code is set as follows:

```
$blue: #3bbfce;
$margin: 16px;

.content-navigation {
  border-color: $blue;
  color:
    darken($blue, 9%);
}

.border {
  padding: $margin / 2;
  margin: $margin / 2;
  border-color: $blue;
}
```

When we wish to draw your attention to a particular part of a code block, the relevant lines or items are set in bold:

```
$red: #3bbfce;
$margin: 16px;

.content-navigation {
  border-color: $blue;
  color:
    darken($red, 18%);
}

.border {
  padding: $margin / 2;
  margin: $margin / 2;
  border-color: $blue;
}
```

Any command-line input or output is written as follows:

```
$ gem install compass
$ compass create <myproject> --sass-dir "sass" --css-dir "css"
  --javascripts-dir "javascripts" --images-dir "images"
```

New terms and important words are shown in bold. Words that you see on the screen, in menus or dialog boxes for example, appear in the text like this: "Click on **I Agree** to accept the license conditions and then click on **Finish** when prompted."

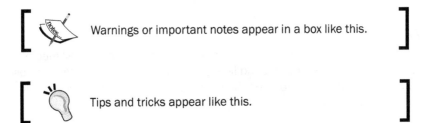

Warnings or important notes appear in a box like this.

Tips and tricks appear like this.

Reader feedback

Feedback from our readers is always welcome. Let us know what you think about this book—what you liked or may have disliked. Reader feedback is important for us to develop titles that you really get the most out of.

To send us general feedback, simply send an e-mail to feedback@packtpub.com, and mention the book title via the subject of your message.

If there is a topic that you have expertise in and you are interested in either writing or contributing to a book, see our author guide on www.packtpub.com/authors.

Customer support

Now that you are the proud owner of a Packt book, we have a number of things to help you to get the most from your purchase.

Downloading the example code

You can download the example code files for all Packt books you have purchased from your account at http://www.packtpub.com. If you purchased this book elsewhere, you can visit http://www.packtpub.com/support and register to have the files e-mailed directly to you.

Errata

Although we have taken every care to ensure the accuracy of our content, mistakes do happen. If you find a mistake in one of our books—maybe a mistake in the text or the code—we would be grateful if you would report this to us. By doing so, you can save other readers from frustration and help us improve subsequent versions of this book. If you find any errata, please report them by visiting http://www.packtpub.com/submit-errata, selecting your book, clicking on the errata submission form link, and entering the details of your errata. Once your errata are verified, your submission will be accepted and the errata will be uploaded on our website, or added to any list of existing errata, under the Errata section of that title. Any existing errata can be viewed by selecting your title from http://www.packtpub.com/support.

Piracy

Piracy of copyright material on the Internet is an ongoing problem across all media. At Packt, we take the protection of our copyright and licenses very seriously. If you come across any illegal copies of our works, in any form on the Internet, please provide us with the location address or website name immediately so that we can pursue a remedy.

Please contact us at copyright@packtpub.com with a link to the suspected pirated material.

We appreciate your help in protecting our authors, and our ability to bring you valuable content.

Questions

You can contact us at questions@packtpub.com if you are having a problem with any aspect of the book, and we will do our best to address it.

Instant SASS CSS How-to

Welcome to *Instant SASS CSS How-to*, where we take you on a journey through using the power of SASS as a CSS pre-processor language, and show you how the power of a little JavaScript, CSS, and Ruby can have a positive impact on your development workflow.

Downloading and installing SASS (Must know)

We're going to kick off the recipes by downloading and setting up SASS ready for use – this will get your system ready to compile SASS files as you create them.

Getting ready

For this recipe you will need a few things – you will need your choice of normal text editor; I normally use TextPad, which is available on a commercial license at `http://www.textpad.com`, although please feel free to use whichever editor you prefer. You will also need a copy of RubyInstaller for Windows, which you can download from `http://www.rubyinstaller.org/downloads`; at the time of writing, the latest version is 1.9.3. If you are a Mac OS X user, you will already have Ruby installed as part of the operating system; Linux users can download and install it through their distribution's package manager.

How to do it...

1. Let's begin by running `rubyinstaller-1.9.3-p286.exe`, and clicking on **Run** when prompted. At the **Select Setup Language** window prompt, select your preferred language – the default is English. At the **License Agreement** window, select **I accept the license** then click on **Next**.

2. At the **Installation Destination and Optional Tasks** window, select **Add Ruby executables to your PATH**, and **Associate .rb and .rbw files with this Ruby installation**:

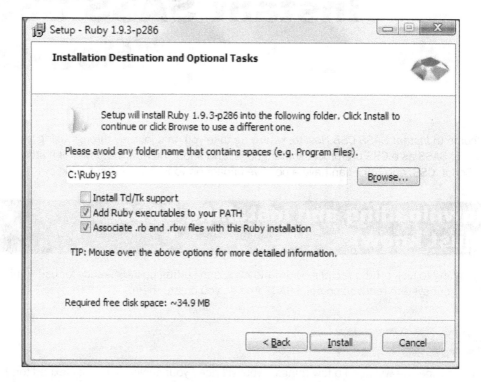

3. Click on **Install**. Ruby will now install, you will see a progress window displayed on the screen while the software is being installed. A dialog window will appear when this is completed. Click on **Finish** to close the window.

4. The next stage is to install SASS. For this, you need to bring up a command prompt, then type `gem install sass` and press *Enter*. Ruby will now go ahead and install SASS – you will see an update similar to the following screenshot:

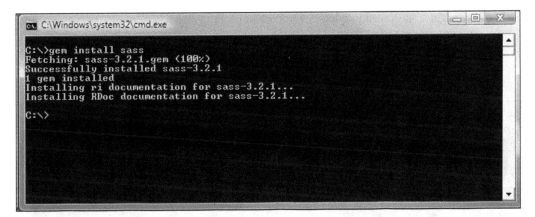

 You may find this takes a short while, with little apparent change on screen; there is no need to worry, as it will still be downloading and installing SASS.

5. Now that SASS is installed, we can go ahead and start creating SASS files. Open up your text editor, add the following lines, and save it as `example1.scss` in a folder called `c:\sass`:

```scss
$blue: #3bbfce;
$margin: 16px;

.content-navigation {
  border-color: $blue;
  color: darken($blue, 9%);
}

.border {
  padding: $margin / 2;
  margin: $margin / 2;
  border-color: $blue;
}
```

Downloading the example code

You can download the example code files for all Packt books you have purchased from your account at `http://www.packtpub.com`. If you purchased this book elsewhere, you can visit `http://www.packtpub.com/support` and register to have the files e-mailed directly to you.

6. We now need to activate the compiler. If you don't already have a session open, bring up a command prompt, and enter the following:

```
sass --watch c:\sass\example1.scss:c:\sass\example1.css
```

If you get a "permission denied" error when running `sass --watch`, then make sure you are running the command prompt as an administrator.

7. This activates the SASS compiler which will then automatically generate a CSS file when any change is made to the SCSS file:

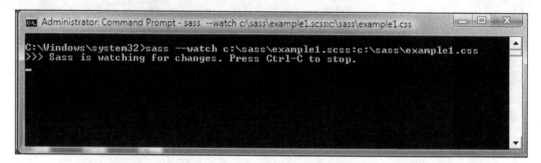

8. As soon as you save the file, the SASS compiler will pick up the change, and update the appropriate CSS file accordingly:

9. If you look in the `c:\sass folder\example1.css` file that has been generated, you will see the resulting CSS, which you can then attach to your project:

```
.content-navigation { border-color: #3bbfce; color:
  #2ca2af; }
.border { padding: 8px; margin: 8px; border-color:
  #3bbfce; }
```

How it works...

In this recipe, we've installed Ruby and SASS, and looked at how to run the SASS --watch command to set the SASS compiler to automatically compile CSS files when you create SCSS files. In this instance, we created a basic SCSS file, which SASS has parsed; it works out where variable "placeholders" have been used, and replaces them with the appropriate value that has been specified at the start of the file. Any variables included in the SASS file that are not subsequently used, are automatically dropped by SASS.

When using Ruby 1.9, SASS is able to automatically determine which character encoding it should use, and will handle this in the same way as CSS (which is UTF-8 by default or a more local encoding for some users). You can change this if needed; simply add @charset "ENCODING-NAME"; at the beginning of the stylesheet, where ENCODING-NAME is the name of a format that can be converted to Unicode.

While the creation of CSS files using this method is simple, it is a manual process that has to be run outside of your text editor. In the next recipe, we'll take a look at how you can add support so you can compile code from within your text editor, using Sublime Text 2 as your example editor.

Adding support to text editors (Must know)

For designers and developers, text editors are a matter of personal preference – there are hundreds available freely, or at low cost. In this exercise, we're going to look at adding support for SASS into Sublime Text 2, although the same workflow principles will apply to similar editors.

Getting ready

For this recipe, you will need to obtain a copy of the shareware application Sublime Text 2, which is available at http://www.sublimetext.com/2 – the latest version at the time of writing is 2.0.1. You will need to purchase a license for continued use – at the time of writing, the cost is USD 59. You will also need to get a copy of the SASS plugin for Sublime Text 2 – you can download either the ZIP or tar package from https://github.com/n00ge/sublime-text-haml-sass/downloads (I will assume you have downloaded the ZIP file, for the purposes of the recipe).

How to do it...

1. Let's begin by installing Sublime Text 2. Double click on the `Sublime Text 2.0.1 Setup.exe` file, and accept all defaults, including selecting the option **Add to explorer context menu**, during the installation.

2. Launch Sublime Text 2 then click on **Preferences**, then **Browse Packages...**. This will open a folder within your profile.

3. Go ahead and extract the contents of the ZIP file you downloaded earlier. Inside it you will find two folders, one called `Ruby Haml` and the other `SASS`. Copy these two folders into the `Packages` folder you opened from within Sublime Text 2, and restart Sublime Text 2.

4. To confirm that all has worked properly, open the `example1.scss` file from the previous recipe in Sublime Text 2; you should see something like the following screenshot:

```
C:\sass\example1.scss • - Sublime Text 2 (UNREGISTERED)

File   Edit   Selection   Find   View   Goto   Tools   Project   Preferences   Help

  example1.scss

1    $blue: #3bbfce;
2    $margin: 16px;
3
4
5    .content-navigation {
6        border-color: $blue;
7        color:
8            darken($blue, 9%);
9    }
10
11   .border {
12       padding: $margin / 2;
13       margin: $margin / 2;
14       border-color: $blue;
15   }

Line 15, Column 2                          Tab Size: 4              SASS
```

How it works...

The SASS support package that you downloaded from Github contains a number of layout instructions to tell Sublime Text 2 how to format SASS code within the browser. It also contains commands that will allow you to build the CSS file from within SASS. If you click on the **Tools** menu, then **Build**, you can initiate the SASS compiler to automatically compile your code, as we did in the previous recipe. It will start the compiler's watch facility, which will then kick in when you make the next change within Sublime Text 2.

There are lots of editors available Sublime Text 2 may not suit your needs, so it is worth looking online and trying a few before finding one that works for you. As an example, for Mac users, you may prefer something like CodeKit, which is available from `http://incident57.com/codekit/index.php`. This already includes support for SASS.

There may be instances where you may prefer to use the command line to create your SASS files though; you may prefer to use a GUI just to compile your code. In the next recipe, we'll take a look at how you can do this, using Scout.

Pre-compiling SASS (Must know)

If you are a web designer, the thought of using the command line may put you off of using SASS; you probably prefer using a tool that has a GUI that can do some or all of the hard work for you. If this is true, then you can use the power of Scout to do the hard work of compiling for you, as you will see in this recipe.

Getting ready

For this recipe, you will need to obtain a copy of Scout. It is available from `http://mhs.github.com/scout-app/`. The latest version at the time of writing is 0.7.1; this is a cross-platform application that will require you to download Adobe AIR. I will assume for the purposes of this exercise that you don't have it installed; you can download it from `http://get.adobe.com/air/`.

How to do it...

1. Double click on the `AdobeAIRInstaller.exe` file to install. Click on **I Agree** to accept the license conditions and then click on **Finish** when prompted.

2. When AIR has been installed, run the `ScoutAppInstaller-0.7.1.exe` file to begin installing Scout. You may find you need to run this as administrator in order to install.

3. You will see the following screenshot. Click on **Continue** to accept defaults and install:

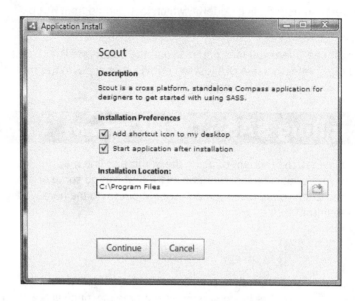

4. Scout is now installed; it will display an initial window, ready to be configured. Click on **+** at the bottom-left of the window then select the c:\sass folder we created earlier. We now need to add in some additional settings, as shown in the following screenshot, the rest can be left as default:

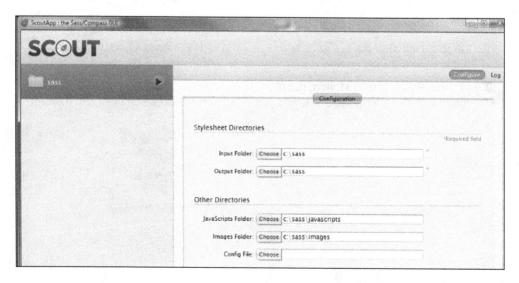

5. Once the additional settings have been entered, these will automatically be saved by Scout. You can then click on the blue and black play button to start the SASS compiler. Any changes you then make to your `.scss` files will be picked up by Scout, which will then update the appropriate CSS file automatically:

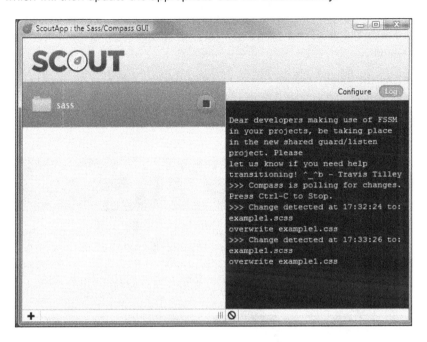

 You may have noticed the warning in the previous screenshot; this is not something to be alarmed about. There is a pending change due in the software from using FSSM to Guard – this is to remove duplication, although there is still some uncertainty about if or when this change may take place.

How it works...

Scout performs much the same process that we looked at earlier in this book; it watches out for any SASS files that it has been made aware of, and will compile them into valid CSS files when a change has been made. The key difference is that while you may have to manually set up a number of different sessions in a command prompt, to watch multiple files, or a single session to watch multiple files, Scout allows you to do this from within one screen. It has the options to add details for watching multiple files or folders, which you can then turn off or on as desired.

There's more...

If you are a Mac or Windows user, and prefer not to use Adobe AIR, then there is an alternative that you can use – LiveReload. It is available at `http://livereload.com/`. This is primarily a Mac application, although a version is available for Windows XP with Service Pack 3 or above. Note though that the latter is an alpha version, so please try it at your own risk; it may not suit everyone!

Now that we have the ability to compile our files, there is one last part we need to look at before we can start writing code – it will be useful to know from within a browser session, which SASS line is being referenced for a particular style. No problem, we can do that using FireSASS, as you will see in our next recipe.

Viewing SASS in a browser (Become an expert)

When you have compiled your SASS files into valid CSS, an important step is to then test to see that it works. If you start seeing unexpected results, you will want to troubleshoot the CSS code. The trouble is, most browsers don't include support to trace back a SASS-compiled style to its original SASS code; we can fix that (at least for Firefox), by using FireSASS.

Getting ready

For this exercise, you will need a copy of Firefox, with Firebug installed. You can get the latter from `http://www.getfirebug.com`.

How to do it...

1. Let's get FireSASS installed. To do this, you need to browse to `https://addons.mozilla.org/en-US/firefox/addon/firesass-for-firebug/`, then click on the **Add to Firefox** button:

 FireSass for Firebug 0.0.9
by nex3

FireSass allows Firebug to display the original Sass filename and line number of Sass-generated CSS styles.

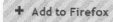 + Add to Firefox

This add-on has been preliminarily reviewed by Mozilla. Learn more

2. Firefox will prompt you to allow it to install. Click on **Allow**, then on **Install Now** on the window that appears. You will need to restart Firefox for FireSASS to complete its installation.

3. To test it, we need to create a SASS file with some example code, and use it within a HTML test page. Go ahead and add the following to a copy of the template from the start of this book, and save it as `example2.html`, within the `c:\sass` folder we created earlier:

```
<body>
<form action="">
    Name: <input type="text" class="input" />
    Password: <input type="password" class="input" />
    <input type="submit" value="This is a button" id="submitfrm"
/>
</form>
</body>
```

4. Add the following to a new SCSS file within Sublime Text 2. Save this as `example2.scss`; you will also need to link this into the `<head>` section of your code:

```
$color-button: #d24444;
#submitfrm {
  color: #fff;
  background: $color-button;
  border: 1px solid $color-button - #222;
  padding: 5px 12px;
}
```

5. Activate the SASS compiler from the command prompt, using the following command:

```
sass --watch c:\sass\example2.scss:c:\sass\example2.css
  --debug-info
```

6. If all is well, you should see the following screenshot when you view the file in your browser:

How it works...

FireSASS works by replacing the line number of the CSS style in use, with that of the line number from the original SCSS file:

```
Style ▾   Computed   Layout   DOM

#submitfrm {                                        example2.scss (line 2)
    background: none repeat scroll 0 0 #D24444;
    border: 1px solid #B02222;
    color: #FFFFFF;
    padding: 5px 12px;
}
```

It relies on the `--watch` function being activated with **--debug-info** enabled. Using the previous example, we can see from the screenshot that the border color calculation of `border: 1px solid $color-button - #222` returned a color of #B02222, which is a slightly darker shade of red than the main button itself. The beauty of this is that no matter whatever color you decide to use, the calculation will automatically return the right shade of color for the border.

Not convinced? Change the `$color-button` variable to something completely different. I've chosen #3bbfce. Now recompile the SASS file in Sublime Text 2 and the result is a nice shade of blue:

Okay, so we've only changed the color for one button in this example – it doesn't matter if you make a change for one button or many; using this code means you only need to change one variable to update any button that uses the same variable in your code.

There's more...

If you look into the folder where you are storing your SASS files, you may notice the presence of a `.sass-cache` folder, inside which there will be one or more `.scssc` files as shown in the following screenshot:

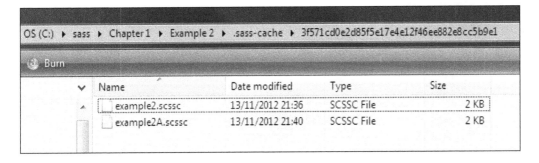

These are cache files, which live in the same folder as your source files by default. They are created by SASS when initially compiling SCSS files. This dramatically speeds up the compilation process, particularly when you have a large number of files to compile. It works even better if styles for a project have been separated into one of these files, which SASS can then compile into one large master file.

Let's move on now, and focus on the library itself. Over the next few exercises, we will look at various elements of the library, beginning with using nested rules.

Using nested rules (Must know)

"Nested rules in CSS...?" How do they work, I hear you ask? Well, it's a very simple principle; your website's stylesheet will have any number of styles within it, all of which will be used in some form or other within your site or application. The trouble is, you are likely have to write duplicate styles in order to reference specific objects on screen. We'll see how you can avoid doing this, as part of the next exercise.

Getting ready

Right – I'm going to throw you in the deep end...no, only joking!

You won't need a great deal for this exercise, as most of it will be completed in your trusty editor, which I hope will be the Sublime Text 2 application we installed earlier in this book. If you don't use Sublime Text 2, then you will need to have an instance of SASS' `watch` command running in the background, to compile code.

You will also need two images, which we will call `tab_a.png` and `tab_b.png`. Copies of these images are available in the code download that accompanies this book. If you prefer to change the colors (as I am no artist!), then please feel free to do so. As long as you keep the same names then this will be fine. You can use a site such as Tabs Generator (`http://www.tabsgenerator.com`) to generate the initial tabs; you are likely to need something like PhotoShop or GIMP to edit them to size.

How to do it...

1. Let's open our text editor, and add the following to a copy of the template from the start of this book, and then save it as `nestedexample.html`:

```html
<body>
  <ul id="menu">
    <li id="home"><a href="index.html"><b>Home</b></a></li>
    <li id="about"><a href="about.html">
      <b>About Us</b></a></li>
    <li id="products"><a href="products.html">
      <b>Products</b></a></li>
    <li id="support"><a href="support.html">
      <b>Support</b></a></li>
    <li id="contact"><a href="contact.html">
      <b>Contact</b></a></li>
  </ul>
</body>
```

2. You'll need to add this to the `<head>` section of your code:

```html
<link rel="stylesheet" type="text/css"
  href="single_one.css">
```

3. Let's now add in the styles to `single_one.scss`, that will turn our unordered list into a menu, beginning with two base mixins:

```scss
@mixin menuposition{
  li a {background-position: right -51px; margin-top:
    -2px; height: 35px;}
}


@mixin menuposition_hover{
  li a b {background-position: left -51px; height: 40px;}
}
```

4. Next come the styles that will control the appearance of our menu:

```scss
#menu {
  padding: 0; margin: 0; list-style: none;

  li {
    float: left; margin-left: 1px; padding-top: 2px;
    a {
      display: block;
      height: 38px;
      line-height: 38px;
      padding: 0 20px 0 0;
```

```
          float: left;
          background: url(tab_a.png) no-repeat right top;
          color: #fff;
          text-decoration: none;

          &:hover {
            background-position: right -51px; margin-top:
              -2px; height: 40px;
          }

          &:hover b {
            background-position: left -51px; height: 40px;
          }
        }

      a b {
        display: block;
        height: 38px;
        float: left;
        padding: 0 0 0 20px;
        background: url(tab_b.png) left top;
        cursor: pointer;
      }
    }
  }
```

5. The last part of the SCSS code assigns the styles to our menu selector IDs:

```
#menu {
  #home {@include menuposition;
    @include menuposition_hover;}
  #about {@include menuposition;
    @include menuposition_hover;}
  #products {@include menuposition;
    @include menuposition_hover;}
  #support {@include menuposition;
    @include menuposition_hover;}
  #contact {@include menuposition;
    @include menuposition_hover;}
}
```

6. If all is well, you should see something similar to the following screenshot, when you save and preview your work in a browser:

How it works...

The key to this exercise is in the #menu block of CSS code – this contains the nested styles that are used by the menu. SASS is able to understand that inner rules will only be applied within the outer rule's selector. This allows you to avoid repetition that you would otherwise get if you were writing styles that are inherited from a parent style. It also means that the code becomes more readable, as the code is in a format that is more logical to the human mind.

There's more...

Some of the more observant of you may have noticed the ampersand (&) being used in this block of code, and one other:

```
&:hover {
  background-position: right -51px; margin-top: -2px;
    height: 40px;
}
```

The ampersand has a special meaning in SASS; it references the parent selector in the same way as the other styles do, but the difference here is that the & character is used when you have special styles such as :hover or :visited. When compiled, the code will look something like the following code snippet:

```
#menu li a:hover {
  background-position: right -51px;
  margin-top: -2px;
height: 40px; }
```

It's time to turn our attention to another part of the library, which is SASSScript. Before we do this, we need to make a small diversion, to look at a small but important part of the library – using comments in SASS – as part of the next recipe.

Using comments in SASS (Should know)

Phew – that last exercise was quite a task! We're going to take a breather and focus on how comments work in SASS. As I am sure you are aware, it is critical to add comments, so you know what something does when you revisit the code at a later date. You'll be pleased to know that this is a very easy exercise in relation to the last one, as comments in SASS work in a similar manner to other programming languages.

Getting ready

All you will need for this exercise is your trusty editor. For the purposes of this recipe, I will assume you are using Sublime Text 2 that we installed earlier in the book. If you don't use Sublime Text 2, then you will also need to have an instance of SASS' `watch` command running in the background, to compile the code.

How to do it...

1. Launch your editor, create a new SASS document, and save it as `comments.scss`. Then add the following example code:

    ```
    .rounded { border-radius: 5px; border: 1px solid #ccc; }
    .widget { @extend .rounded; border-color: darkred; }
    .bright-widget {@extend .widget; border-color: #cc99ff; }
    ```

2. Let's now add in some comments. Alter the previous code, so it looks like the following code snippet:

    ```
    // this is our base style, that would be used across all widgets
    .rounded {border-radius: 5px; border: 1px solid #ccc; }

    /* Here we're extending our style, to give our first
     * widget a nice dark red color. */
    .widget {@extend .rounded; border-color: DarkRed; }

    /*! Our second widget needs a different color - this
     * time we'll go for a brownish red color. */
    .bright-widget {@extend .widget; border-color: #370000; }
    ```

This produces the following in Sublime Text 2:

3. Save your work, then press *Ctrl* + *B* to compile the code. SASS will generate the following code, as shown in the following screenshot:

How it works...

Adding comments to SASS files is very easy, it is no different to adding comments to code, when using PHP or JavaScript for example. However, there are some features you need to be aware of:

- Have you noticed how, when the code was compiled, the comments disappeared from the base widget style? Single-line comments are always stripped out from compiled SASS code, whereas multiline comments (such as the ones at lines 5-6 and 10-11 in the previous code) are kept:

```
.rounded, .widget, .bright-widget {
  border-radius: 5px;
  border: 1px solid #ccc; }

/* Here we're extending our style, to give our first
 * widget a nice dark red color. */
.widget, .bright-widget {
  border-color: DarkRed; }

/* Our second widget needs a different color - this
 * time we'll go for a brownish red color. */
.bright-widget {
  border-color: #370000; }
```

- There may be occasions where you don't want to put in multiline comments - if you add an exclamation mark (as shown in line 14 of the SCSS file), the comment will be interpolated, and SASS will render this in the CSS output, even in compressed output modes as you will see in the *Controlling output in SASS (Must know)* recipe, later in this book. You don't need to use the exclamation mark option when using multiline comments, although if used, it won't affect the output.

Now that we've seen how comments work, it's time to turn our attention to something more in-depth. Let's take a look at how you can use functions and operators within SASS, starting with a look at SASS Script.

Getting interactive with Script (Become an expert)

If you are using SASS, then there is a likelihood that you are familiar with using the command line, either in a Windows, Apple, or UNIX based environment. Although you can use something like Scout or Compass.app to help take some of the pain out of compiling SCSS files, it is worth trying out the command line – there is a hidden gem available in the form of interactive SASS. Let's take a look at how this works, as part of this next exercise.

Getting ready

All you will need for this exercise is a terminal or command prompt, depending on which environment you use.

How to do it...

1. Let's make a start by calling up a command prompt or terminal window, entering sass -i at the command prompt, and then pressing *Enter*:

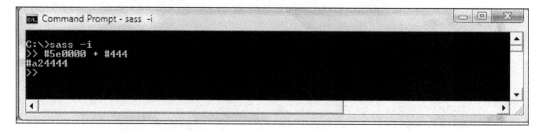

2. You will see from the previous screenshot that I've already entered in a command. Go ahead and try it out; a quick look at ColorHexa (http://www.colorhexa.com) shows #5e0000 to be a brownish-red color. Adding it to #444 (a dark gray) gives a nice shade of brown, in the form of #a24444.

3. Now try entering in margin-left: 5px + 8px/2px...oops! It's come back with an error. I am guessing that you may have been expecting 9px as the answer. (If you were expecting 6.5px, then sorry, that's not correct either!)

4. Okay, now try entering lighten(#99ccff, 20%), you should get back #3399ff; a check on ColorHexa shows a nice shade of light-blue, which is expected.

5. To finish, let's now enter in adjust-color(blue, $lightness: -20%, $hue: 20deg) – this renders #330099 as the result, which is a solid shade of purple.

6. At this point, press *Ctrl + D* to exit out of the session and then close the window.

How it works...

Right – you're probably thinking "How I can use this in my work...?"

It's a good question – let me explain. Interactive SASS is not meant to be an all-singing, all-dancing part of the library. Think of it as a way of validating your calculations, particularly when working with colors and/or numbers (such as sizes). Interactive SASS allows you to enter in any number of simple calculations, and it will render the results on screen. You won't be able to enter in large mixins, but if you need to confirm what a simple calculation would render, then this is perfect.

In particular, notice the error shown in step 3? While the calculation itself is perfectly valid, Interactive SASSScript doesn't like the `margin-left:` text at the start, hence the error. If you're wondering why `6.5px` is wrong, it is because certain operators are prioritized before others. In this example, the division is done before addition, so 8 px divided by 2 px gives 4 px, plus 5 px gives 9 px as the answer.

Its real power comes in step 5 – the calculation is a bit of a mouthful, so having the ability of Interactive SASS available is a great help to confirm the expected result. It also means that if you wanted to reduce the complexity down to a single color value, then you can. It is entirely up to you.

Let's move on and turn our attention to a different part of the library. We'll be taking a look at using CSS-3 directives within SASS; we will come back to using functions later in the book.

Using CSS-3 directives in SASS (Must know)

The mere mention of the word "directive" may seem intimidating to some people, particularly when coding. In reality, they are perfectly harmless! The directive you are likely to use the most is that of `@import`, although this is just a small part of what is available. SASS supports all standard CSS-3 directives such as `@media`, as well as some of its own. In this exercise, we're going to look at three directives, namely `@extend`, `@import`, and `@include`, as part of building some dialog boxes that you could use in your projects.

Getting ready

For this recipe, we're going to need some suitable icons for each dialog box. There are dozens available online for you to choose from. One such place is the Open Icon Library Project (`http://openiconlibrary.sourceforge.net`). You will need three icons in total; one for the alert dialog, one for information, and one for the error dialog.

You will of course need your text editor as well. For the purpose of this example we will be using Sublime Text 2.

How to do it...

1. Let's make a start by creating our template (from the start of the book) for displaying the alerts. Create a new document and save it as `css3rules.html`. Add the following code in the `<head>` tag area:

    ```
    <link rel="stylesheet" type="text/css"
      href="css3rules.css">
    ```

2. Add the following code in the `<body>` area:

```
<body>
   <div class="info">Information you need to know</div>
   <br /><br />
   <div class="alert">Alert you triggered</div>
   <br /><br />
   <div class="error">Error with our code</div>
</body>
```

3. We now need to add some styling to our alerts – without it, they won't look very good! Go ahead and add the following code snippet to a new SCSS document, and save it as `css3rules.scss`. We will begin with the base style required for our alert dialog box:

```
@import "css3mixins";


body {
   color: #444444;
   font-family: 'Lucida Grande',Verdana,Arial,Sans-Serif;
   font-size: 14px;
}


.base { @include rounded-top(5px); text-align: left;
   padding: 20px 20px 5px 75px; width: 200px;
      height: 50px; }
```

4. Next comes the first of three types – the alert dialog:

```
.alert { @extend .base;

   background: #fff6bf url(images/exclamation.png) 5% 50% no-

   repeat; border: 2px solid #ffd324; }
```

5. The second one is the style required for an information dialog:

```
.info {
   @extend .base;
   background: #F8FAFC url(images/information.png) 5% 50%
      no-repeat;
   border: 2px solid #B5D4FE;
}
```

6. The last style is required for displaying the error dialog:

```
.error { @extend .base;
   background: #FFBFBF url(images/error.png) 5% 50%
      no-repeat;
border: 2px solid #FF2424; }
```

7. Our final step is to add in the mixin – this controls the border edge. Add the following code snippet to a new file, and save it as `css3mixins.scss`:

```
@mixin rounded-top($radius) {
  border-radius: $radius;
  -moz-border-radius: $radius;
  -webkit-border-radius: $radius;
}
```

8. Save all of your work and then preview it in a browser. If all has gone well, you should see something similar to the following screenshot:

How it works...

In this exercise, we've looked at two components of the CSS-3 directives functionality available within SASS – the @import and @extend directives. The former allows us to bring in (or import) content from multiple sources into one file. When SASS compiles the files, it will produce one CSS file that contains all of the imported styles within it. This has the benefit of removing the need for multiple requests to the server, while still maintaining the ability to separate our work into smaller, more manageable chunks.

 You will notice that we use use of the @import directive a fair amount throughout this book.

The second directive is that of `@extend` – think of it as a form of inheritance. It tells SASS to include the base mixin by default. However, it doesn't just include it as additional styles within the same block, thereby leading to unnecessary code bloat, but to create a base style that applies to all styles that subsequently inherit it:

```
.base, .alert, .info, .error { width: 200px; height: 50px;
   border-radius: 5px; -moz-border-radius: 5px;
   -webkit-border-radius: 5px; padding: 20px 20px 5px 75px;
   text-align: left; }

.alert { background: #fff6bf url(images/exclamation.png) 5%   50%
   no-repeat; border: 2px solid #ffd324; }
```

There's more...

There is a wealth of functionality you can use within SASS, and which we've not been able to cover here in this book. It is worth looking at the documentation available online to familiarize yourself with what is possible. A good example is the `@media` directive. This behaves much in the same way as CSS does, but SASS allows you to embed it into nested styles, in a similar way to how we've used `@extend` in our example.

Let's move on now and look at another part of the SASS library – control directives. I'm sure you've all used functions such as `foreach`, `while`, and `until` when programming code? Well, you can do something similar in SASS. I'll show you how, using the power of social media and `@each` as our example.

Controlling output in SASS (Must know)

How many times, when you've visited sites, have you seen any number of social media icons at the bottom of postings? I certainly have and that's saying something, for the 3000-plus bookmarked sites I've bookmarked over the years! (I think it went as high as 12,000+ sites before I trimmed out the duplicates, chuckle!).

Normally you might embed icons in the page for them and build up similar styles for each – this could potentially be a real bore, as the styles won't change from icon to icon and it is likely to produce a lot of code! Now, how about producing the same amount of compiled code, but from less than 20 lines of code? We'll see how, as part of the next exercise.

Getting ready

You'll need your trusty text editor. Ideally this should be Sublime Text 2, as we will be compiling SCSS code. We'll also need some social media icons, for which there are plenty of sources available on the Internet. As an example, you could try the ones available at GoSquared (`https://www.gosquared.com/resources/gosocial`). As well as getting the icons, you will need to rename each icon you use to the format `icon-XXXXXX.png`, where XXXXXX is the name of the social network, such as LinkedIn. I will assume we are using these icons during the exercise, and that they have been suitably renamed.

How to do it...

1. We'll begin by creating our template. Go ahead and create a new document, and add the following code in the `<head>` tag area. Then save it as `socialmedia.html`.

```
<link rel="stylesheet" type="text/css" href="socialmedia.css">
<link href='http://fonts.googleapis.com/
   css?family=Macondo' rel='stylesheet' type='text/css'>
```

2. Add the following code in between the `<body>` tags:

```
<body>
   <a class="icon-deviantart" href="http://www.deviantart.com">
     deviantart</a>
   <a class="icon-digg" href="http://www.digg.com">digg</a>
   <a class="icon-facebook" href="http://www.facebook.com">
     facebook</a>
   <a class="icon-forrst" href="http://www.forrst.com">forrst</a>
   <a class="icon-lastfm" href="http://www.last.fm">last.fm</a>
</body>
```

3. Next up we'll need our SCSS code, so create a new SCSS file in Sublime Text 2, and save it as `socialmedia.scss`. Add the following code:

```
@each $socnet in facebook, digg, deviantart, forrst,
   lastfm {
   a.icon-#{$socnet} {
     padding: 5px 40px 20px; color: #8B4513;
       display: block;
     background: url('images/icon-#{$socnet}.png')
       no-repeat left top; width: 100px;
       font-family: 'Macondo', cursive;
     font-weight: bold; font-size: 24px;
       text-decoration: none;
     &:hover {
       text-decoration: underline;
     }
   }
}
```

4. If all is well, you will see the following screenshot when you preview your work in a browser (we've added a Google Web font, to give the icons some style!):

How it works...

Although this exercise was deliberately designed to be simple, it serves up a perfect example of how you can cut down the amount of code you need to write, while still maintaining the same result.

Here, we've used the power of @each to loop through each name specified, and to create the appropriate styles using the rules specified:

```
padding: 5px 40px 20px;
color: #8B4513;
display: block;
background: url('images/icon-#{$socnet}.png') no-repeat left top;
width: 100px;
font-family: 'Macondo', cursive;
font-weight: bold;
font-size: 24px;
```

The beauty of this is that it cuts down the amount of repetitive code you have to write in your stylesheet. Provided the same format is used throughout, then each icon will receive the same styles (apart from the name of the image, naturally). To see how effective this is, have a look at the compiled code in Sublime Text 2. My copy listed 64 lines of styling code, compared to the 16 we've had to write. That's a real difference, isn't it?

 A small word of advice. This is a very powerful part of the library; the developers recommend that this should only be used when creating mixins, and not in the course of day to day styling as they require a fair amount of flexibility.

Let's move on, and turn our attention to another part of the library, and one I am sure you will be using regularly – mixins. I'll show you how over time, you can build up a library of reusable code that can be dropped in at a moment's notice.

Creating and using mixins (Must know)

Mixins – we've used a few of these in some of the exercises so far in this book, but, what are they and how do they work?

Mixins are probably the single most useful part of SASS. They allow you to build partial blocks of code, which you can literally mix-in (hence the name) as part of larger style sheets. The key benefit of using them is that they can help remove duplication of code, in much the same way as functions work. I will show you how they work in the next exercise, as part of styling the ubiquitous button.

Getting ready

All we'll need in this recipe is our trusty text editor. If you are using Sublime Text 2 (which I hope you are), you can use the SASS compiler that we hooked in from earlier in the book.

How to do it...

1. Let's make a start by creating a new HTML document, adding the code template from the start of this book, and saving it as `creatingmixins.html`. You will need to update the CSS stylesheet link thus:

   ```
   <link rel="stylesheet" type="text/css"
     href="creatingmixins.css">
   ```

2. Add the following in between the `<body>` tags:

   ```
   <body>
     <a href="#" class="buttonclass">my button</a>
   </body>
   ```

3. We now need to add some styles, so create a new SCSS document, and save it as `creatingmixins.scss`. Add the following code, beginning with the three mixins:

   ```
   @mixin gradient($from, $to) {
     background: -webkit-gradient(linear, left top, left
       bottom, color-stop(0.05, $from), color-stop(1, $to));
     background: -moz-linear-gradient(center top, $from 5%,
       $to 100%);
     filter: progid:DXImageTransform.Microsoft.gradient
       (startColorstr='#{$from}', endColorstr='#{$to}');
   }
   ```

```scss
@mixin rounded-corners($radius) {
  -webkit-border-radius: $radius;
  -moz-border-radius: $radius;
  border-radius: $radius;
}

@mixin box-shadow($top, $left, $blur, $spread, $color) {
  -webkit-box-shadow: inset $top $left $blur $spread
    $color;
  -moz-box-shadow: inset $top $left $blur $spread $color;
  box-shadow: inset $top $left $blur $spread $color;
}
```

4. Next comes the main style class for the button, so go ahead and add the following to your SCSS file:

```scss
.buttonclass { @include gradient(#fe1a00, #ce0100);
  @include rounded-corners(6px);
  @include box-shadow(0px, 1px, 0px, 0px, #f29c93);
  background-color:#fe1a00; border:1px solid #d83526;
  display:inline-block; color:#ffffff; font-family:arial;
  font-size:15px; font-weight:bold; padding:6px 24px;
  text-decoration:none; text-shadow:1px 1px 0px #b23e35;
}
```

We'll also include styles for hovering and making the button active:

```scss
.classname:hover { @include gradient(#ce0100, #fe1a00);
  background-color:#ce0100; }


.classname:active { position:relative; top:1px; }
```

5. If all is well, you will see the following button when saving and previewing your work in a browser:

How it works...

Although at first glance it might seem a lot of code to style a button, but a closer look will reveal that most of the code comes from the three mixins that we've included. Mixins are blocks of code that can be imported into a new or existing CSS stylesheet, in much the same way as you might reuse programming code. SASS is clever enough to only compile in those styles that are being used by the HTML code to which they relate.

The key to understanding the previous code is in the `@include` keyword. When compiling, SASS will bring in the CSS styles from the mixin whenever it sees a mixin placeholder, as shown by the lines highlighted in the following code snippet:

```
.classname {
  background: -webkit-gradient(linear, left top, left bottom,
    color-stop(0.05, #fe1a00), color-stop(1, #ce0100));
  background: -moz-linear-gradient(center top, #fe1a00 5%,
    #ce0100 100%);
  filter: progid:DXImageTransform.Microsoft.gradient
    (startColorstr='#fe1a00', endColorstr='#ce0100');
  -webkit-border-radius: 6px;
  -moz-border-radius: 6px;
  border-radius: 6px;
  -webkit-box-shadow: inset 0px 1px 0px 0px #f29c93;
  -moz-box-shadow: inset 0px 1px 0px 0px #f29c93;
  box-shadow: inset 0px 1px 0px 0px #f29c93;
  background-color: #fe1a00;
  border: 1px solid #d83526;
  display: inline-block;
  color: #ffffff;
  font-family: arial;
  font-size: 15px;
  font-weight: bold;
  padding: 6px 24px;
  text-decoration: none;
  text-shadow: 1px 1px 0px #b23e35; }


.classname:hover {
  background: -webkit-gradient(linear, left top, left bottom,
    color-stop(0.05, #ce0100), color-stop(1, #fe1a00));
  background: -moz-linear-gradient(center top, #ce0100 5%,
    #fe1a00 100%);
  filter: progid:DXImageTransform.Microsoft.gradient
    (startColorstr='#ce0100', endColorstr='#fe1a00');
  background-color: #ce0100; }

.classname:active {
  position: relative;
  top: 1px; }
```

There's more...

"This is all good, but how is it going to be useful to me...?"... I hear you ask. The answer to that question is simple – in the three mixins you have the beginnings of a code library that can be reused within your projects as many times as you need, and that you can build up over time. SASS will only ever import styles that are referenced within the HTML, so there is no danger of code bloat. You can also separate your SCSS code into several documents; SCSS will import each and create one master document as part of compiling the code, thereby reducing the number of requests made to the server.

Taking the code we've used here further, you could include functions within the mixin (as we've covered in this book), to work out the right shades of color to use – all with the use of parameters as part of calling in the mixins. This should mean you only need to pass in one color.

Ah-ha! Perfect timing – it just so happens that the next exercise is about functions. Although we're going to play with some text, the same principles could easily apply to styling objects such as buttons. Let's take a look and see how functions work in SASS.

If you would like to see an example of what could be achieved with styling buttons using SASS, then take a look at `http://jaredhardy.com/sassy-buttons/`, there are some good examples there!

Building functions within SASS (Must know)

I'm sure that as a seasoned developer, you will be used to working with functions and operators in code...what if I said you could do the same with CSS? Yes, you heard correctly – with CSS. Well, you can; the power of SASS means that you could potentially create a whole color theme for something like WordPress, from one base color. Let's take a look how, as part of our next recipe.

Getting ready

All we need for this recipe is our text editor. For the purposes of this recipe, I will assume that you are using Sublime Text 2. If you don't use Sublime Text 2, then you will need to have an instance of SASS' `watch` command running in the background, to compile code.

How to do it...

1. Let's begin by opening Sublime Text 2, and adding the following code snippet to a copy of the template we created at the start of this book. Save it as `sassfunctions.html`:

```html
<body>
  <h1>Heading 1</h1>
  <h2>Heading 2</h2>
  <h3>Heading 3</h3>
  <h4>Heading 4</h4>
  <h5>Heading 5</h5>
</body>
```

2. You'll also need to add the following code snippet in, this will incorporate our compiled styles:

```html
<head>
  <meta http-equiv="content-type"
    content="text/html; charset=utf-8" />
  <link rel="stylesheet" href="sassfunctions.css"
    type="text/css" >
</head>
```

3. We now need to add in our styles. Go ahead and create a new SCSS document, then add the following styles, starting with our `firefox-message` mixin, and base variables:

```scss
@mixin firefox-message($selector, $message) {
  #{$selector}:before { content: $message; }
}


$firefox-greeting: "Hi Firefox users! This is a....";
$mainColour: #631;
$h1Size: 4em;
$removemargin: -20px;
```

4. Let's now add in each of the H styles, from 1 to 5:

```scss
h1 { @include firefox-message("&", "Hi Firefox users!
  This is a...."); font-size: $h1Size;
  color: transparentize($mainColour, 0.3);
}
h2 { @include firefox-message("&", $firefox-greeting);
  color: lighten($mainColour, 5%);
  margin-top: $removemargin; font-size: $h1Size * .8;
}
h3 { @include firefox-message("&", $firefox-greeting);
  color: lighten($mainColour, 10%);
```

```
        margin-top: $removemargin; font-size: $h1Size * .6;
    }
    h4 { @include firefox-message("&", $firefox-greeting);
        color: lighten($mainColour, 15%);
        margin-top: $removemargin; font-size: $h1Size * .4;
    }
    h5 { @include firefox-message("&", $firefox-greeting);
        color: lighten($mainColour, 20%);
        margin-top: $removemargin; font-size: $h1Size * .2;
    }
```

5. If all is well, you should see something similar to the following screenshot, when saving and previewing your work in a browser:

Hi Firefox users! This is a....Heading 1

Hi Firefox users! This is a....Heading 2

Hi Firefox users! This is a....Heading 3

Hi Firefox users! This is a....Heading 4

Hi Firefox users! This is a....Heading 5

How it works...

In this recipe, we've used three pieces of functionality from the library – color functions, string interpolation, and operators.

String interpolation is a simple but very powerful function in SASS. It allows you to use placeholders within your code, so that when a string is passed through to a function, SASS will replace that placeholder with the desired value as part of compiling the code.

Operators work in a similar way to other languages – here, we've used them to work out the font-size value that should be used for each style. For example, based on an H1 style set at 4em, an H3 font size will work out as 0.6 x 4em, or 2.4em.

The `lighten` and `transparentize` functions are part of SASS' library of functions for working with color. The former will lighten a given color by the specified amount, and the latter will make a color more transparent by the amount given. A key thing to note is that SASS will normally leave color formatting alone; the exception to this is when using HSL colors, which are automatically output as hex values and HSLa values are shown as RGBa equivalents. You may therefore find RGBa values appearing in your code, in a similar fashion to what we've used for the H1 style rule in this exercise:

```
    color: rgba(102, 51, 17, 0.7);
    font-size: 4em; }

    h1:before { content: "Hi Firefox users! This is a...."; }
```

It won't make any difference to the outcome, although some people find it easier to use, as it is not always easy to tell what a hex color value is!

There's more...

This is a really powerful part of SASS, which, if used correctly can significantly reduce the amount of values that you have to work out, such as colors for a theme. It does require you to take care over how you do – to misquote a well-known phrase, "measure twice, and drill a hole once", or in this case, "calculate twice, and then write once..." – you get the idea...

To show you how important it is to take care with this part of the library, a perfect example arose when writing this demo; I used this rule to create my H1 style:

```
    h1 { @include firefox-message("&", $firefox-greeting);
      color: transparentize($mainColour, 0.3);
      font-size: $h1Size;
    }
```

This pulled in the firefox-message mixin, we will learn more about these later:

```
    @mixin firefox-message($selector, $message) {
      #{$selector}:before { content: $message; }
    }
```

This compiled to the following code, notice the deliberate error?

```
    h1 { color: rgba(102, 51, 17, 0.7); font-size: 4em; }
      h1 h1:before {
        content: "Hi Firefox users! This is a...."; }
```

In case you didn't spot it, you can't use a double H1 attribute when referencing the content rule. To fix this, you need to pass an ampersand instead of the H1 attribute:

```
    h1 {
      @include firefox-message("&", $firefox-greeting);
      color: transparentize($mainColour, 0.3);
      font-size: $h1Size;
    }
```

SASS understands that the whole rule will automatically apply to each style. The & sign tells SASS to use each selector that is passed and to assign the :before pseudo-selector when creating the rule for displaying the text.

Altering output style (Should know)

So far, we've looked at a number of different parts of the SASS library, to see how it can help you write more efficient CSS. There's one thing that we've not touched on though, and this is something about which I am very particular: making sure the CSS stylesheet looks presentable! Most developers should do this as a matter of course, it can become a real pain if you're managing more than 2,000 lines of CSS styling, such as in a WordPress theme. What if you could set the style *automatically*? You can and we'll see how in the next recipe.

Getting ready

For this recipe you will need your text editor. Here, I'm using Sublime Text 2, although you can use an alternative if you prefer. You will also need Scout up and running, which we installed earlier in this book. While you can use the command line route to control the output style, Scout makes it much easier to achieve!

How to do it...

1. Let's make a start by creating a folder in which to store our compiled CSS files. Call it `example output` and store it under `C:\sass`, for the purposes of our recipe.

2. We now need to configure Scout to scan for changes in our SCSS files. Open up Scout and change the `Input` and `Output` folders to `c:\sass\example output`.

3. We also need to set the output modes as well. Set the **Environment** option to `Development` and the `Output Style` to `Compressed`.

4. Now that Scout is configured, let's go ahead and start it. To do so, click on the **Log** button on the right-hand side of the window, and then on the Play [▶] button which changes to a Stop [■]button:

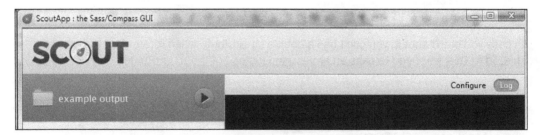

5. We can now create our SCSS file. Open up Sublime Text 2 and add the following code snippet, saving it as `example output - compressed.scss`. The code itself won't actually do anything, but is enough to demonstrate the different output styles:

```
/* Example - compressed output */
.errorOne { font-size: 10px; font-weight: 400; }
```

```
.errorTwo { font-size: 20px; font-weight: 200; }
.errorTwo { @extend .errorOne; color: blue; }
```

6. Save the file and watch Scout to confirm it has picked up the changes and generated the CSS file accordingly. This will be in our example output folder that we created earlier:

Name	Date modified	Type	Size
.sass-cache	18/11/2012 11:56	File Folder	
example output - compressed.css	18/11/2012 11:20	Cascading Style S...	1 KB
example output - compressed.scss	18/11/2012 11:20	SCSS File	1 KB

7. Let's take a look at the output generated in the CSS file:

```
.errorOne,.errorTwo{font-size:10px;
  font-weight:400}.errorTwo{font-size:20px;
  font-weight:200}.errorTwo{color:blue}
```

8. This is an example of the compressed style – let's go back to Scout and choose **Expanded** as a different style. Switch back to Sublime Text 2 and save a copy of the SCSS code as example output - expanded.scss. Scout should automatically compile the file, and output the following code:

F:\SASS Book\Code\Chapter 2\output\example output - expa...

File Edit Selection Find View Goto Tools Project Preferences Help

example output - expanded.css

```
1    /* Example - expanded output */
2    /* line 2, example output - expanded.scss */
3    .errorOne, .errorTwo {
4      font-size: 10px;
5      font-weight: 400;
6    }
7
8    /* line 7, example output - expanded.scss */
9    .errorTwo {
10     font-size: 20px;
11     font-weight: 200;
12   }
13
14   /* line 12, example output - expanded.scss */
15   .errorTwo {
16     color: blue;
17   }
```

Line 17, Column 2   Tab Size: 4   CSS

How it works...

Notice the difference in styles between the two files? SASS makes it very easy to output your code in any one of the four different styles. You can choose from **Expanded**, **Compressed**, **Compact**, or **Nested**. All you need to do is to change the **Output Style** option in Scout to your preferred choice, then stop and restart Scout by clicking on the play/stop button as shown in step 4 of this recipe. Scout takes care of compiling the code in the chosen format for you.

There's more...

I mentioned earlier that we would use Scout for this recipe – with very good reason. It is possible to compile the code with the appropriate output style set, but it is more of a manual process.

If you prefer to compile via the command line, then you can use the `-style` switch to achieve the same result. This is how you would compile the code using the compressed format:

```
sass --watch --style compressed style.scss:style.css
```

The trouble is, you will have to enter this at the start of each session, unless you add it to a batch file (or Mac equivalent), and run it. This can be a pain, particularly as the earlier command will only watch for the named file!

You can also achieve the same result using Compass (we will see more of Compass later in the book). As part of using Compass, you can add in an option to the `config.rb` file, similar to the following code snippet:

```
# You can select your preferred output style here (can be overridden
via the command line):
output_style = :compressed #:expanded or :nested or :compact or
:compressed
```

Using this option means you would use Compass' version of `watch`, instead of SASS'. The highlighted change would apply to all files in the same project folder, whereas the earlier SASS command only applies to the file being watched. Overall, Scout is more flexible, even if it is not the speediest!

Okay, so far we've focused our attention on functionality that is available with the core SASS library. Let's go a little further afield now, and look at how you can use pre-built external libraries such as Bourbon within your code, using a classic jQuery-based sliding panel as our example.

Using a pre-built mixin library (Should know)

Now, for those of you partial to a little whiskey (yes, Irish or Scottish – it doesn't matter), you might be sorely disappointed; Bourbon isn't just the name of a variety of whiskey, but it is also that of a pre-built SASS library you can freely use in your projects, in a similar way to Compass (of which we will see more, later in this book). Let's take a look at how we can use SASS to build up the CSS needed to create a sliding door demo. The inspiration for this is based on a tutorial published by SypreStudios, available at `http://spyrestudios.com/demos/sliding-panel-fixed/`

Getting ready

For this recipe, we're going to need a few things, along with our trusty text editor:

- A copy of the Bourbon mixin library, which is available at `http://bourbon.io/`.
- Two images – a plus sign and a cross; each should be about 20 px square in size. There are images available within the code download for this book, otherwise there will be images available for download online. For the purposes of this recipe, I will assume you've used the images provided in the code download for this book.
- Some dummy text from the Lipsum generator available at `http://www.lipsum.net` – you will need three paragraphs' worth of content (two for the background and one for the panel).

How to do it...

1. Let's make a start by installing the Bourbon mixin library. Bring up a command prompt and type in `gem install bourbon`:

```
Command Prompt

C:\>gem install bourbon
Fetching: thor-0.16.0.gem (100%)
Fetching: bourbon-2.1.2.gem (100%)
Successfully installed thor-0.16.0
Successfully installed bourbon-2.1.2
2 gems installed
Installing ri documentation for thor-0.16.0...
Installing ri documentation for bourbon-2.1.2...
Installing RDoc documentation for thor-0.16.0...
Installing RDoc documentation for bourbon-2.1.2...

C:\>_
```

2. Once this has completed, type in `bourbon install` at the command prompt, which will create a number of files and folders in a folder called `bourbon` at the root of `C:`. These are required for Bourbon to be used correctly later in this recipe.

3. In the `bourbon` folder we've just created, go ahead and add an additional folder called `projects`; we'll use this to store our SCSS files that use Bourbon. In the `projects` folder, add a subfolder called `css` – this will store our compiled CSS files.

4. Okay, now that we have our basic workflow set up, let's start creating some code. Create a new folder and call it `sliding door demo`, then go ahead and add a new HTML document, saving it in this folder as `slidingdoor.html`.

5. We now need to add the framework code for our sliding panel. Let's begin by adding in the following code to the `<header>` area of our HTML document:

```
<title>Vertical Sliding Info Panel With jQuery</title>
  <link rel="stylesheet" href="style.css" type="text/css"
    media="screen" />
  <script type="text/javascript"
    src="http://code.jquery.com/jquery-1.8.3.min.js">
  </script>
```

6. Add in the following script immediately below the reference to jQuery:

```
<script type="text/javascript">
$(document).ready(function(){
  $(".trigger").click(function(){
    $(".panel").toggle("normal");
    $(this).toggleClass("active");
    return false;
  });
});
</script>
```

7. You will have noticed a reference to `style.css` in the previous code. Go ahead and create a new document with that name. This is where our compiled styles will reside.

8. Next, let's add in some dummy text immediately after the `<body>` tag, so that we have a valid page on which to host our sliding panel. This uses the dummy text generated from `Lipsum.net`:

```
<div id="container">
  <h1>Vertical Sliding Info Panel With jQuery</h1>
  <p>Lorem ipsum dolor sit amet, consectetur adipiscing
    elit. <a href="#">9te get eros libero</a>. Fusce
    tempus quam sit amet erat mollis a fermentum nibh
    imperdiet. Fusce iaculis sapien in turpis 9te get
    porta. Donec tincidunt gravida tortor, vel dignissim
    augue convallis sit amet. Aliquam auctor ornare
    accumsan. Cras convallis elit tincidunt arcu 9te ge
```

egestas. Mauris interdum fringilla nisi. Cras a
dapibus lectus. Praesent blandit ullamcorper ornare.
Nam hendrerit sollicitudin urna non ultricies.
Phasellus condimentum auctor risus, at accumsan
tellus tempor vel. Nunc mattis eleifend dolor at
adipiscing.</p>
</div>

9. Now that we have the background text in place, let's go ahead and add in the text for our sliding panel. Add in the following code immediately after the closing `<div>` tag for `<container>`:

```
<div class="panel">
  <h3>Sliding Panel</h3>
  <p>Here's our sliding panel/drawer made using jQuery
    with the toggle function and some CSS3 for the
    rounded corners</p>
  <p>Ut purus metus, fermentum vitae pulvinar vel,
    elementum eget nulla. Pellentesque posuere, enim ut
    dapibus vestibulum, leo nunc porttitor neque, sed
    pulvinar orci sem eleifend sapien. Nullam at odio
    nibh, eu pharetra ipsum. Pellentesque eget ante nec
    ante consequat ullamcorper a vitae mauris. Integer
    lacus lorem, sollicitudin vulputate posuere at,
    commodo a sapien. Vivamus lobortis vehicula
    imperdiet. Donec a congue tortor. Fusce augue tortor,
    pretium pharetra pellentesque ornare, laoreet nec
    sapien. Ut eget magna tellus. Pellentesque posuere
    accumsan condimentum.</p>
  <div style="clear:both;"></div>
</div>
<a class="trigger" href="#">infos</a>
```

10. Okay, so the code is now in place – it looks a little untidy though, as it doesn't have any styling in place. We're going to fix this by creating our SASS styles. Create a new SCSS file and save it as `style.scss` in the `projects` folder which we created earlier.

11. Let's now add in the styles, beginning with the reference to Bourbon and the two mixins:

```
@import "bourbon/bourbon";

@mixin demofont ($textcolor, $textsize, $textfamily) {
  font-family: $textfamily; font-weight: 700;
    color: $textcolor; font-size: $textsize; }

@mixin linkdecor ($position, $bordercolor, $textstyling,
  $display) {
  position: $position; border: 1px solid $bordercolor;
```

```
text-decoration: $textstyling; display: $display; }
```

12. We next need to add in some basic styles for the page:

```
body { @include demofont(#666, 14px, $georgia);
  background: #1a1a1a; text-align: left; width: 700px;
  font-size: 14px; margin: 0 auto; padding: 0; }
a:focus { outline: none; }
h1 { @include demofont(#9FC54E, 34px, $verdana);
  letter-spacing: -2px; padding: 20px 0 0; }
h3 { @include demofont(#fff, 14px, $verdana);
  letter-spacing: -1px; text-transform: uppercase;
  margin: 0; padding: 8px 0 8px 0; }
img { float: right; margin: 3px 3px 6px 8px;  padding:
  5px; background: #222222; border: 1px solid #333333; }
p { color: #cccccc;  line-height: 22px;
  padding: 0 0 10px;  margin: 20px 0 20px 0; }
```

13. Next comes the styles for the main container on the page:

```
#container { clear: both; margin: 0; padding: 0; }

#container a { @include demofont(#fff, 16px, $verdana);
  @include border-radius(0px 20px 0px 20px); float:
  right; background: #9FC54E; border: 1px solid #9FC54E;
  text-decoration: none; letter-spacing: -1px;
  padding: 20px; margin: 20px;

  &:hover { @include demofont(#fff, 16px, $verdana);
    @include border-radius(0px 20px 0px 20px);
    float: right; background: #a0a0a0; border: 1px solid
    #cccccc; text-decoration: none; letter-spacing:
    -1px; padding: 20px;
  }
}
```

14. We need to add in the styles for the slide-out panel. Add these in immediately below the #container style from the previous step:

```
.panel {
  @include border-radius(0px 20px 20px 0px);
    position: absolute; top: 50px; left: 0;
    display: none; background: #000000;
    border: 1px solid #111111; width: 330px;
    height: auto; padding: 30px 30px 30px 130px;
    opacity: .85; filter: alpha(opacity=85);

  p { margin: 0 0 15px 0; padding: 0; color: #cccccc; }
}
```

15. Finally here are the styles for the trigger:

```
a.trigger {
  @include demofont(#fff, 16px, $verdana);
  @include border-radius(0px 20px 20px 0px);
  @include linkdecor(absolute, #444, none, block);
  top: 80px; left: 0; letter-spacing: -1px;
  padding: 20px 40px 20px 15px; background: #333333
    url(images/plus.png) 85% 55% no-repeat;

  &:hover {
    @include demofont(#fff, 16px, $verdana);
    @include border-radius(0px 20px 0px 20px);
    @include linkdecor(absolute, #444, none, block);
    top: 80px; left: 0; letter-spacing: -1px;
      padding: 20px 40px 20px 20px;
      background: #222222 url(images/plus.png) 85% 55%
      no-repeat;
  }
}

a.active.trigger { background: #222222
  url(images/minus.png) 85% 55% no-repeat; }
```

16. Save your SCSS file. Then open up a command prompt as administrator, and enter the following command:

```
sass --watch c:/bourbon/projects:./bourbon/projects/css -r
  ./bourbon/lib/bourbon.rb
```

17. If the file has correctly compiled, then you will see a CSS file within your projects/css folder which we created earlier. Copy this over to your sliding door demo folder.

You may see the following error when compiling the code, it can be ignored (only for the moment as I will explain more, later in the book):

WARNING: border-radius mixin is deprecated and will be
   removed in the next major version release.

on line 3 of C:/bourbon/css3/_border-
   radius.scss, in `border-radius'

from line 39 of c:/bourbon/projects/style.scss

---

18. Preview your work. If all is well, you should see something similar to the following screenshot, where the **infos** link has already been clicked, and the icon against it is replaced with a red cross:

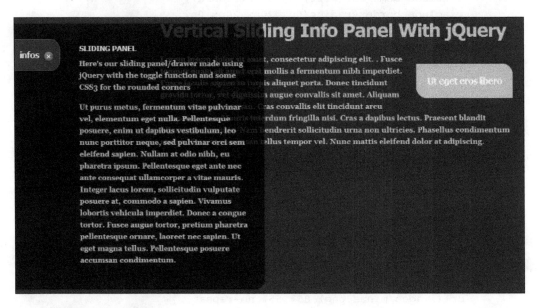

How it works...

Phew - that was some recipe! Let's take a look at what we've achieved. Although it seems a lot of code, we've used jQuery to animate a div in and out, depending on whether the trigger [◉] icon has been clicked. The jQuery code in itself is very small; most of the work was in styling the page!

In the SCSS code, we've used a number of SASS features to help us style the code. Notice the `@import` call at the top of the code? This tells SASS to use the Bourbon library we installed earlier, and allows us to use the `border-radius` mixin. We then have two mixins – one for setting font styles, and another for styling some of the links. We've also used nesting on some of the styles, including using the `&` keyword to correctly include pseudo styles, such as `:hover`. We also have a `border-radius` mixin from the Bourbon library; remember the comment made earlier about the warning message you may have when compiling the code? While the code will still work, it is worth noting that vendor prefix support has changed since the Bourbon library was first written. Specific vendor entries for `border-radius` will be removed from the library as most browsers support `border-radius` by default.

The other important part of this recipe is in the compiling of the SCSS styles, which used the following command:

```
sass --watch c:/bourbon/projects:./bourbon/projects/css
  -r ./bourbon/lib/bourbon.rb
```

As of version 3.01 of SASS, there is no need to pass the -r parameter when using –watch with Bourbon.

It may look a little confusing, but it breaks down into the following: it is using the Sass `sass` command to watch (–watch) a folder called `c:\bourbon\projects`, which will put compiled files into a subfolder called `css`, and to do that it requires (–r) the bourbon ruby file `bourbon.rb`. It's important to learn this, as it is very likely that you will need to use a similar command when including other pre-built mixin libraries in the future.

Now that we've begun to look at mixins, it's a good point to pause for a moment, and consider an important concept that would be wise for you to master when using SASS – developing your own style of writing mixins.

Writing mixins – developing a style (Must know)

Okay – you're probably thinking I'm going mad at this point; why do we need to develop a style for writing mixins? Don't worry, all will be revealed as part of this recipe!

Getting ready

For this recipe, you won't actually need anything, we're just going to look at some theory. Although you may want to play with code from this book, using the principles we'll go through as a basis for developing your own style.

 This recipe should be treated as part of a number of steps that you can take to help develop your own style. We will use examples to illustrate each stage, although they may not necessarily do much when compiled!

How to do it...

1. Let's make a start with our first guideline – a module should contain a unit of code in a partial. For example, a file could contain code for buttons, another for forms, and a third for typography.

 Partials are blocks of source code that are inserted into generated CSS files. The underscore character tells SASS not to produce a corresponding CSS file for the block of code.

2. Our second guideline is around the output of that code. A module should never contain code that would compile into CSS code. This will limit the contents of the module to mixins, variables, and functions.

3. Taking this further, our third guideline is that while a module may contain a number of mixins or functions, there should always be a primary mixin which is responsible for outputting the resulting CSS code.

4. Our next guideline recommends that we should use the primary mixin name as the name for our module. For example, if our module contains a primary mixin for buttons, then we should name the partial as `buttons.scss`.

5. If we use variables in our modules, we should also give consideration to making sure that they have a default set. This will allow us to override these variables in a theme stylesheet, or when we reuse the module in future projects.

6. Finally – and in conjunction with our first guideline – almost all CSS for a project should be written in a modular style. This will help you with reusing styles across stylesheets in a project, or to reuse code between different projects.

How it works...

The beauty of working with SASS and CSS is that there are no hard and fast rules about presentation, it is all about developing your own style. The previous guidelines are not meant to be set in stone, they are designed to help structure your code and steer you towards a more modular approach, so that you can begin to reuse your code in future projects.

Downloading and installing Compass (Should know)

So far, we've had a look at how to write our own mixins, as well as importing and using pre-written mixin libraries. We should not forget the most popular mixin library that is available for use with SASS though, which is Compass. We're going to turn our focus to installing support for it, as part of the next recipe.

Getting ready

For this recipe, all you will need is a command prompt.

How to do it...

1. Let's get started by firing up a command prompt, and entering the following command:

```
gem install compass
```

You should see the following screenshot:

```
C:\>gem install compass
Successfully installed compass-0.12.2
1 gem installed
Installing ri documentation for compass-0.12.2...
Installing RDoc documentation for compass-0.12.2...

C:\>_
```

2. That's all – it's very easy! Sorry to disappoint you if you were expecting more...

> If you find the installation bombs with an error regarding RDOC documents already being installed for Compass, then all you need to do is to rename the `rdoc` folder in `C:\Ruby193\lib\ruby\gems\1.9.1\doc\compass-0.12.2` to something different and then rerun the installation. The fault occurs because a folder for RDOC documents for Compass will have been created when Ruby was installed, but documents haven't been added. The install for Compass doesn't overwrite this folder by default.

How it works...

This is a very easy recipe, all we have done is run a command to install Compass. Ruby applets such as Compass come in the form of gems, which can be installed directly into Ruby, using Ruby's `gem install` procedure.

There's more...

Although the recipe is very easy to complete, the project provides an option to list the steps you need to take to install Compass and set up your first project, which you can see at `http://compass-style.org/install/`. The steps are very similar to the ones we've been through in this recipe. It does give you the option to choose how you want to set up your Compass project, and will pipe out the commands you need to run to create that project environment.

If we use the following folder structure of `sass` for scripts, `javascripts` for JavaScripts, `images` for images, and `css` for stylesheets, it would give the following command; as shown in the screenshot and command example:

```
$ gem install compass
$ compass create <myproject> --sass-dir "sass" --css-dir "css"
  --javascripts-dir "javascripts" --images-dir "images"
```

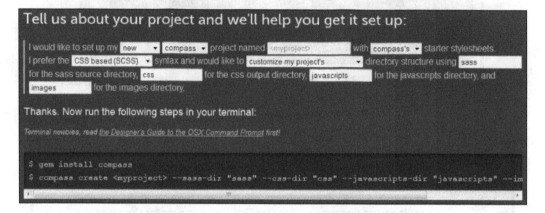

 The previous commands are for a UNIX environment; replace $ with C:\ or your chosen drive letter for use in Windows.

There are other options available using this tool – if you feel comfortable using the command line, then this is worth trying it out. If not, then you can always use a GUI-based application, such as Scout, which we covered earlier in this book.

Now that we have Compass installed, let's move on and turn our attention to using its functionality. In this and the next recipe, we're going to look at two elements that you are likely to use often, which is creating image sprites and using vendor prefixes.

Creating sprites using Compass and SASS (Become an expert)

One of the best ways to reduce server requests, and consequently response times for a site is to create sprites from your images. You could easily use a website to do this, or you can use the power of Compass to do this for you. We're going to look at how to do this using some credit card images, which could easily appear on an e-commerce site.

Getting ready

For this recipe, you will need some suitable images that are a maximum of 32 px square. I have used a selection of 12 credit card images which are available at `http://www.smashingmagazine.com/2010/10/21/free-png-credit-card-debit-card-and-payment-icons-set-18-icons/`. You will of course also need your text editor and Scout up and running.

How to do it...

1. Let's make a start by creating a folder called `c:\compass`, then open up a command prompt, and add the following command. We will use the default folders for the purpose of this recipe:

   ```
   $ compass create compass --sass-dir "sass" --css-dir "css"
      --javascripts-dir "javascripts" --images-dir "images"
   ```

2. In the `compass` folder we've just created, you will find a folder called `sass`. Go ahead and create a new subfolder in there called `cards` and drop in our 12 images.

3. We need to next fire up Scout, as it will be easier to compile the code this way. When open, click on **+** at the bottom-left corner of the Scout window, and add the following settings, as seen in the following screenshot, and leave all others as default. When complete, click on the **Stop** button to start scanning that folder for changes:

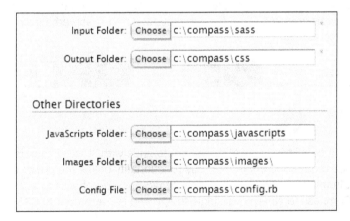

4. Switch to Sublime Text 2, then create a new document and add the following code, saving it as `imagesprites.scss`:

   ```
   @import "compass";

   $cards-layout: horizontal;
   $cards-spacing: 5px;
   $cards-sprite-base-class: ".cards-icons";
   ```

```
@import "cards/*.png";
@include all-cards-sprites;
```

5. The code should look like the following screenshot within Sublime Text 2:

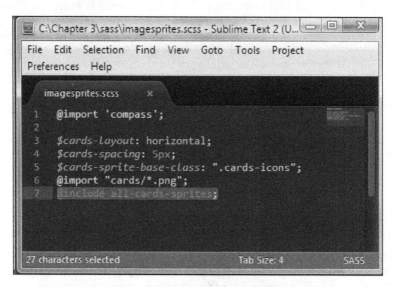

6. At the time of saving Scout should kick in, and create the sprite for you. If all is well, you will see an auto-generated PNG file appear in the `sass` folder, similar to `cards-sad556f86f6.png`. Opening it up will reveal something similar to the following screenshot:

How it works...

Although this might be a little tricky at first to get to grips with, it is worth persevering – the three lines of code required to implement this functionality belies the power of creating sprites using Compass. In this example, we've collected together a number of images of the same size, and used Compass to generate a single image and the appropriate CSS to allow us to reference each image.

The resulting CSS will include a base style that references the newly created image, followed by individual styles that tell the browser which part of that image to use, as shown in the following extract from the `imagesprites.css` file:

```
/* line 130, cards/*.png */
.cards-icons, .cards-cirrus-curved-32px, .cards-delta-curved-32px,
    .cards-direct-debit-curved-32px, .cards-discover-curved-32px,
```

```
    .cards-maestro-curved-32px, .cards-mastercard-curved-32px,
    .cards-paypal-curved-32px, .cards-solo-curved-32px,
    .cards-switch-curved-32px, .cards-visa-curved-32px,
    .cards-visa-electron-curved-32px,
    .cards-western-union-curved-32px {
    background: url('/cards-sad556f86f6.png') no-repeat;
}

/* line 60, ../../Program Files/Scout/vendor/gems/gems/compass-
    0.12.2/frameworks/compass/stylesheets/compass/utilities/
    sprites/_base.scss */
.cards-cirrus-curved-32px {
    background-position: 0 0;
}
```

Using sprites in your web pages reduces the number of server requests and decreases response times – each subsequent reference to the image calls it from the server cache. You could even get fancy and store it in the local storage area of a compatible browser. This will eliminate any server requests, if done with care! There is a small proviso though with using Compass to create sprites – size and number play an important part in image selection. If Compass deems you've used too many, then it will automatically switch from the default 8-bit format to a higher format, with the associated increase in size and load times. At this stage, it may be preferable to use an external service instead, such as SpritePad (http://www.wearekiss.com/spritepad).

Let's move on, and take another look at this veritable swiss-army knife of a library –vendor prefix support. Compass is often recommended as a good place to start when learning SASS. We're going to look at vendor prefix support, as part of building a simple form in the next recipe.

Using vendor prefixes and Compass (Become an expert)

As previously mentioned, Compass is a real swiss-army knife of a library, in that it contains all kinds of functionality that you can use. In this recipe, we're going to look at how you can use Compass to automatically include the relevant vendor prefixes, using a simple example of styling three buttons in a simulated form.

Getting ready

For this recipe, all we need is our text editor and Scout (there is a reason for using this, which I will explain later). I will assume you are using Sublime Text 2, which we installed earlier in this book. You will need to have the hex values for three colors to hand – you may already have some in mind, but if not, you can use an online site such as `http://www.colorhexa.com/` to choose the hex codes for three colors.

How to do it...

1. We need to store our project somewhere, so let's create our workspace. Open up a command prompt and type the following command:

    ```
    compass create vendor --bare --sass-dir "sass" --css-dir
      "css" --javascripts-dir "javascripts"
      --images-dir "images"
    ```

2. This gives us a confirmation message that our project has been created. To confirm, open up Windows Explorer, and look for your vendor folder which is at the root of `C::`

Name	Date modified	Type	Size
.sass-cache	17/11/2012 16:54	File Folder	
css	17/11/2012 16:54	File Folder	
sass	17/11/2012 18:27	File Folder	
config.rb	17/11/2012 15:41	Ruby File	1 KB
vendorprefixes.html	17/11/2012 17:46	Firefox HTML Doc...	1 KB

3. Let's now go ahead and create the template file – open Sublime Text 2 and add the following code to a copy of the template from the beginning of the book, and then save it as `vendorprefixes.html`:

    ```html
    <body>
      <form action="demo_form.php">
        Username: <input type="text" name="username" />
        <input type="submit" value="Submit" class="redbutton"/>
      </form>
      <p>
        <form action="demo_form.php">
          Username: <input type="text" name="username" />
          <input type="submit" value="Submit" class="rbbutton"/>
        </form>
      <p>
      <form action="demo_form.php">
    ```

```
Username: <input type="text" name="username" />
<input type="submit" value="Submit" class="grbutton"/>
</form>
</body>
```

4. You'll also need to add this to the `<head>` section, so we can incorporate the compiled styles:

```
<head>
<link href='http://fonts.googleapis.com/css?family=Cookie'
  rel='stylesheet' type='text/css'>
<link rel="stylesheet" type="text/css"
  href="css/vendorprefixes.css">
</head>
```

5. We now need to provide the styles for the buttons. There's a good chunk of code required for this, so we'll go through it block by block, beginning with two source mixins:

```
@import "compass";

@mixin gradient($first, $second) { background: $second;
  background: -webkit-gradient(linear, left top, left
  bottom, from($first), to($second)); background:
  -moz- linear-gradient(top, $first, $second); filter:
  progid:DXImageTransform.Microsoft.gradient(
  startColorstr='$first', endColorstr='$second');
}
```

6. We now need to add in the mixin that will do the real work – this is the base for each button:

```
@mixin button_base {
  @include border-radius(.5em);
  @include box-shadow(0 1px 2px rgba(0, 0, 0, 0.2));
  display: inline-block; zoom: 1; *display: inline;
  vertical-align: baseline; margin: 0 2px; outline:
    none; cursor: pointer; text-align: center;
  text-decoration: none; font: 14px 'Cookie', Arial,
    Helvetica; padding: .5em 2em .55em;
    text-shadow: 0 1px   1px rgba(0,0,0,.3);
    font-size: 20px; padding: .20em 1.0em .20em;
  &:hover { text-decoration: underline; }
  &:active { position: relative; top: 1px; }
}
```

7. This next mixin controls the styling and color to be used, as well as styles for hovering and marking the button as an active link:

```
@mixin defined_color ($color1) {
  color: lighten($color1, 10%); border: solid 1px
  darken($color1, 27%); background: darken($color1, 13%);
  @include gradient(darken($color1, 48%),
  darken($color1, 24%));
  &:hover { background: darken($color1, 24%);
  @include gradient(darken($color1, 27%),
    darken($color1, 17%)); }
  &:active { color: darken($color1, 34%);
  @include gradient(darken($color1, 24%),
    darken($color1, 4%)); }
}
```

8. Now that we have defined our button styles, we need to pull all of the mixins together, so we can style each button accordingly:

```
input.redbutton { @include button_base;
  @include defined_color(#fae7e9); }

input.rbbutton { @include button_base;
  @include defined_color(#BC8F8F); }

input.grbutton { @include button_base;
  @include defined_color(#DAA520); }
```

9. Save your work and preview it in a browser. If all is well, you should see something like the following screenshot:

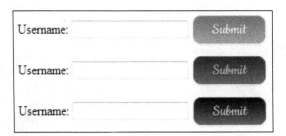

How it works...

The key to how this recipe works lies in how we've split off styles for each button into two parts – the base style, and the décor that defines each button's individual color. Think of it as baking a cake – the base style is the sponge layer, which will be the same throughout. We're making each resulting end style individual by adding different icing (or in this case, colors) on top.

To achieve this, we've used two mixins from the Compass library, `border-radius` and `box-shadow`. SASS then replaces each call for each mixin with the appropriate code from the Compass mixin library, during compilation:

```
input.redbutton {
  -webkit-border-radius: 0.5em;
  -moz-border-radius: 0.5em;
  -ms-border-radius: 0.5em;
  -o-border-radius: 0.5em;
  border-radius: 0.5em;
  -webkit-box-shadow: 0 1px 2px rgba(0, 0, 0, 0.2);
  -moz-box-shadow: 0 1px 2px rgba(0, 0, 0, 0.2);
  box-shadow: 0 1px 2px rgba(0, 0, 0, 0.2);
  display: inline-block;
  zoom: 1;
  *display: inline;
  vertical-align: baseline;
  margin: 0 2px;
  outline: none;
```

When designing this tutorial, I was tempted to use a third style from the Compass library, `linear-gradient`. However, I wasn't happy with how it worked, as it didn't appear to like using the `darken()` functions as part of the library call, and I didn't want to have to add a number of additional variables to get around this. I added my own version instead, it does serve to highlight that while there are lots of mixins available online, they won't necessarily fit your needs. Sometimes it is better to write your own!

Let's move on and turn our attention to using Compass to build another piece of functionality that is very popular – the ubiquitous slider that you will have seen on dozens of sites around the Internet.

Building a slider using Compass (Become an expert)

If you browse through the Internet regularly, it is very likely that you will have come across many sites that use a content slider in some form or other. In this recipe we're going to take a look at how you can use Compass to style such a slider.

Getting ready

For this recipe, you will need a copy of the downloaded code for this book, which is available at the Packt website. However, space constraints mean we're not going to be able to reproduce it here in full, so you will need to refer to a copy from the code download. You will also need a copy of the open-source FlexSlider library which you can download from `https://github.com/woothemes/FlexSlider/zipball/master`. You will also need your choice of text editor, as well as the Scout application running. I'm going to assume you will be using Sublime Text 2 for the purposes of this recipe.

How to do it...

1. Let's make a start by setting up a folder for our work. For the purposes of this recipe, I will assume you've called it `slider`, and that it is stored at the root of `c:`.

2. Next, let's go ahead and create a Compass project. Bring up a command prompt and enter the following command from root of `c:`:

   ```
   compass create slider --bare --sass-dir "sass" --css-dir
     "css" --javascripts-dir "javascripts"
     --images-dir "images"
   ```

3. This will create the base project, and so we now need to copy some files into this folder. Go ahead and open up the ZIP archive you downloaded from `woothemes.com` for this project, and extract the following files:

   - From the `\images` folder, copy this `bg_direction_nav.png` to `c:\slider\images`
   - From the `\demo\images` folder, copy the four `kitchen_*` images to `c:\slider\images`
   - From the `\demo\js` folder, copy `jquery.mousewheel.js`, and `modernizr.js` to `c:\slider\js`
   - From the root of the archive, copy `jquery.flexslider.js` to `c:\slider\js`

4. From the code download available for this book, copy the following:

   - Copy `Flexslider.scss`, `style.scss`, and `fsbase.scss` to `c:\slider\scss`
   - Copy `index.html` to `c:\slider`

5. We now need to get Scout running. Open up Scout, and let's add in the watch for our `slider` folder using the following details:

   - Input Folder: `c:\slider\sass`
   - Output Folder: `c:\slider\css`
   - JavaScripts Folder: `c:\slider\js`

- ❏ Images Folder: `c:\slider\images`
- ❏ Config File: `c:\slider\config.rb`
- ❏ Environment: set this to **Production**

6. When Scout is configured, click on the **Play** button to start the watch process. It should automatically create new CSS files in the `c:\slider\css` folder. A quick check in the folder confirms this:

Name	Date modified	Type	Size
flexslider.css	30/11/2012 23:04	Cascading Style S...	3 KB
fsbase.css	30/11/2012 21:46	Cascading Style S...	2 KB
style.css	30/11/2012 23:04	Cascading Style S...	5 KB

7. Go ahead and preview your work in a browser. You should see something like the following screenshot:

Slider exercise using FlexSlider

How it works...

If you look back at the main `index.html` file, the process for building a slider is in fact very simple. We've included calls to instances of jQuery (via Google's CDN), Modernizr (for fall-back support), a MouseWheel library (for mousewheel support in the slider), and of course FlexSlider itself. It then focuses on an unordered list (lines 19 to 24), around which we've added some extra markup, similar to what you might add in a production website.

We then add in calls to the FlexSlider library towards the end, which is where the magic happens to turn our unordered list into a slider. We've then used Compass to help style the resulting output into something recognizable as a slider. A look through the CSS code should also reveal some of the Compass features that we used earlier in the book. Did you recognize the mixins in `flexslider.scss`, the `@import` statements in `style.scss`, as well as the nested styles in `fsbase.scss`?

There's more...

This recipe illustrates perfectly how SASS can play nicely with other libraries. After all, we're producing what is effectively normal CSS. If you find the CSS from some libraries such as Modernizr doesn't work so well, then all you should need to do is hive this CSS off into a separate file, if you do experience problems using it with SASS.

Now, I'm sure there will be one question you're asking: what about using SASS in something like a CMS system? Absolutely, this is where it can really help, particularly where themes (such as WordPress) can run up to a couple thousand lines! In the last two recipes of this book, we will take a look at how you can use SASS in a CMS system such as WordPress, and see how you can use SASS to cut down your development time.

Using SASS with Wordpress (Become an expert)

In this and the next recipe, we're going to take a look at using the Bones theme in WordPress, which incorporates SASS, and will save us a great deal of time. We will work through installing it, familiarizing ourselves with the theme structure, and make some changes to see how it works.

Getting ready

For this recipe, you're going to need a few things, in addition to your choice of text editor:

- ▶ A working installation of WordPress – either on a local or remote server (sorry but this won't work for `Wordpress.com` sites, as it doesn't support the use of the `@import` tag, which we will be using in this recipe). For this recipe, I will assume you are using a local copy of WordPress (version 3.4.2 at time of writing), hosted through WAMP.

- ▶ A copy of the open source WordPress Bones theme, which you can download from `http://themble.com/bones/`.

- ▶ A working installation of Scout, configured to watch the `scss` folder in the Bones theme (as indicated in the recipe).

How to do it...

1. Let's begin by extracting the theme from the ZIP archive you've downloaded. Inside you will see a folder with a name similar to `eddiemachado-bones-53d7155`; extract it to your WordPress theme folder, and rename it to `bones`.

2. Activate the Bones theme in the theme admin area in WordPress, in the normal manner.

3. Navigate to `\bones\library` within your WordPress theme folder in Windows Explorer. Inside, you will find a number of folders; one of this is called `scss`, which contains the SASS files for the Bones theme.

 If you're expecting to edit the `style.css` file, but don't find any code, don't worry. Bones has been developed to work with the contents of the `\library` file as its CSS source. The main `style.css` file in the root of the theme is there to purely allow WordPress to recognize the theme in the admin gallery only.

4. Go ahead and open up `_base.scss` from within the `scss` folder, in Sublime Text 2, and look for the `#content` style on or around line 245.

5. Alter the code as shown:

```
#content { margin-top: 2.2em; background-color: #D5AEAB;
    margin-left: auto; margin-right: auto; width: 60%; }
```

6. Save the changes, then copy the three recompiled files from the `scss` folder to the `css` folder, as we did in step 3, and refresh your browser window. It will have shrunken the main content area to 60 percent of the width, and added a purple background.

7. Okay, let's do the same with the header. Look for `.header{}` on or around line 153 in `_base.scss`. Alter the style to the following line:

```
.header { margin-left: auto; margin-right: auto; width:
    62.5%; }
```

8. Save your work, then copy the `style.css` file over to the `css` folder, in the same way as we did in step 7. Refresh your browser view and notice how the header has been moved into the center, in the same way we did for the content area.

9. Now we're going to make two more changes to the style sheet. First, look for `.footer`, on or around line 819, and alter it as follows:

```
.footer { clear: both; margin-left: auto;
    margin-right: auto; width: 62.5%; }
```

10. Finally, let's add in a slight adjustment to the text in the footer – it looks a little cramped and could use some color:

```
.copyright { background-color: #EEE; padding: 5px; }
```

11. If everything has worked, we'll end up with something similar to the following screenshot, when you preview it in a browser:

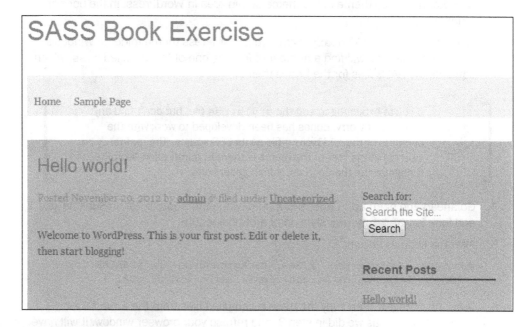

How it works...

In this recipe, we've installed a copy of the Bones theme into a working installation of WordPress and begun to navigate around the SASS partial files, and made some minor changes. I know, before you say anything, it's certainly not going to win any prizes for style! But it highlights a useful point; it is perfectly possible to use SASS in a CMS environment. Indeed, it is almost essential in some respects, if only to manage the large number of lines of code effectively.

We've pulled in a number of concepts that we've covered throughout this book, such as mixins, functions, partials, importing, and more. It may seem somewhat complicated, but if you spend any time developing in WordPress, it will be worth spending time just going through the code, so that you can learn how the theme works. It is important to bear in mind though that a fair amount of the functionality you might otherwise have expected to see, won't be there – the developers did this intentionally as they wanted the theme to act as a base for your own development. After all, it's easier to add functionality, then to take it away!

We have now reached the final recipe in this book – don't worry, it's a nice easy one! We're going to stay with the theme of working with WordPress, and look at how you can use Compass to provide additional vendor support for CSS3 styles.

Using Compass in WordPress (Become an expert)

We've been through a real whistle stop tour of SASS and seen how it works – let's finish on a nice easy demo, which looks at how you can use Compass to provide vendor prefix support to our Bones theme in WordPress.

Getting ready

For this recipe, you will need your trusty text editor (preferably Sublime Text 2). You will also need Scout up and running, and configured to scan the `\bones\library` folder in your WordPress theme folder. We'll also need the Bones theme from the previous recipe. For the purposes of this recipe, I will assume that the settings remain unchanged from the previous task.

How to do it...

1. Let's make a start by opening up a copy of the `_mixins.scss` file in the `\bones\library\scss` folder within the Bones theme. This contains all of the CSS3 mixins that we will work on.

2. On or around line 18, add in the following line to call in Compass:

    ```
    @import "compass";
    ```

3. Move down to the border-radius mixin, that starts on or around line 161:

```
150    /*********************
151    BORDER RADIUS
152    *********************/
153
154    /*
155    I totally rewrote this to be cleaner and easier to use.
156    You'll need to be using Sass 3.2+ for these to work.
157    Thanks to @anthonyshort for the inspiration on these.
158    USAGE: @include border-radius(4px 4px 0 0);
159    */
160    |
161    @mixin border-radius($radius...) {
162        // defining prefixes so we can use them in mixins below
163        $prefixes:       ("-webkit", "-moz", "-ms", "-o",   "");
164      @each $prefix in $prefixes {
165        #{$prefix}-border-radius: $radius;
166      }
167
168      border-radius: $radius;
169    }
```

4. Let's comment out this mixin, as we're going to move to using the Compass version.

5. Compass' version of border-radius is the same format as the one used in the Bones theme, so there is no need to change it in the Bones code. Go ahead and save your work. Check in the \bones\library\scss folder, you should find a freshly compiled style.css file. Copy this (and the other two – login.css and ie.css) to the css folder underneath \bones\library.

6. To check that it has worked, open up the style.css file within \bones\library\ css, and look for the .buttons class on or around line 638. You should find the compiled code for border-radius.

7. Let's go for something little more involved – we will replace the box-shadow mixin, currently in use at line 204 with the version from Compass.

8. Comment out the line at 287, and replace it with the following line (note that the order is reversed in comparison to that used by Bones):

```
@include box-shadow(lighten($bones-blue, 16%) inset 0 0
    3px);
```

9. Save and recompile your work, then copy the updated CSS file to \bones \library\css. If you open up the style.css file from within that folder, you will find the box-shadow style in use at line 824.

How it works...

Although we've only scratched the surface with the changes we've made, it opens up a wealth of possibilities of what you can do in WordPress using Compass, or even any other similar mixin library. The same principle was used in both cases in this recipe – we've inserted a reference to Compass, found the mixin we're going to replace, and then removed the original. We've either left the original reference further down the _mixins.scss file as is, or altered it to fit in with the format used by Compass, then saved and recompiled the file.

One question that you may ask though is – why do it? The answer is simple: you could spend time maintaining vendor prefixes, which will come and go over time, or you could get someone to do it for you! There's no real technical necessity to do this, it is entirely up to you how you manage it, depending on what fits in best with your work environment.

The different versions of SASS – an explanation

If you read the official documentation, you will see a mention made of two different versions of SASS. So, you're probably thinking: what's the difference? The main one is SCSS, with the older one known as SASS (hence the name).

SCSS, or "Sassy CSS" as it is often known, is the primary version used by most developers today. It uses the file format that ends in .scss. The older format, SASS, is still supported, although is not the primary syntax. It is suited to those who prefer conciseness over similarity to CSS3. The real irony though is that the file extension you would assume is being used for the primary syntax isn't – it's the older format that uses .sass as its extension!

 For the purposes of this book, although we may use the name SASS interchangeably, we will be referring to the newer syntax that ends in .scss.

Are you ready to get stuck in? Before you do, there's one small thing we need to do, which relates to the template being used for each of the exercises in this book.

A template for the book recipes

Many of the exercises in this book will follow the same format. I would recommend saving a copy of the following code as a template, to help you when you start working on the exercises throughout this book (with the exception of some of the early tasks, which will be slightly different):

```
<!DOCTYPE html>
<html>
```

```
<head>
  <script>
    <meta http-equiv="content-type" content="text/html;
      charset=utf-8" />
    <link rel="stylesheet" type="text/css" href="XXXXXX.css">
  </script>
</head>
<body>
</body>
</html>
```

We've taken a look at a number of recipes, to show you how you can get started with using SASS in your pages. This is only just the start of what you can achieve using SASS – there is a whole world out there to explore. I hope you've enjoyed working through the recipes, just as much as I have enjoyed writing this book!

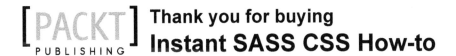

Thank you for buying
Instant SASS CSS How-to

About Packt Publishing

Packt, pronounced 'packed', published its first book "*Mastering phpMyAdmin for Effective MySQL Management*" in April 2004 and subsequently continued to specialize in publishing highly focused books on specific technologies and solutions.

Our books and publications share the experiences of your fellow IT professionals in adapting and customizing today's systems, applications, and frameworks. Our solution based books give you the knowledge and power to customize the software and technologies you're using to get the job done. Packt books are more specific and less general than the IT books you have seen in the past. Our unique business model allows us to bring you more focused information, giving you more of what you need to know, and less of what you don't.

Packt is a modern, yet unique publishing company, which focuses on producing quality, cutting-edge books for communities of developers, administrators, and newbies alike. For more information, please visit our website: www.packtpub.com.

Writing for Packt

We welcome all inquiries from people who are interested in authoring. Book proposals should be sent to author@packtpub.com. If your book idea is still at an early stage and you would like to discuss it first before writing a formal book proposal, contact us; one of our commissioning editors will get in touch with you.

We're not just looking for published authors; if you have strong technical skills but no writing experience, our experienced editors can help you develop a writing career, or simply get some additional reward for your expertise.

Ext JS 4 Web Application Development Cookbook

ISBN: 978-1-84951-686-0   Paperback: 488 pages

Over 110 easy-to-follow recipes backed up with real-life examples, walking you through basic Ext JS features to advanced application design using Sencha Ext JS.

1. Learn how to build Rich Internet Applications with the latest version of the Ext JS framework in a cookbook style

2. From creating forms to theming your interface, you will learn the building blocks for developing the perfect web application

3. Easy to follow recipes step through practical and detailed examples which are all fully backed up with code, illustrations, and tips

HTML5 Video How-To

ISBN: 978-1-84969-364-6

Over 20 practical, hands-on recipes to encode and display videos in the HTML5 video standard

1. Learn something new in an Instant! A short, fast, focused guide delivering immediate results.

2. Encode and embed videos into web pages using the HTML5 video standard

3. Publish videos to popular sites, such as YouTube or VideoBin

Please check **www.PacktPub.com** for information on our titles

PUBLISHING

Instant LESS CSS
Preprocessor How-to

Instant LESS CSS Preprocessor How-to

ISBN: 978-1-78216-376-3

Practical, hands-on recipes to write more efficient CSS, with the help of the LESS CSS Preprocessor library

1. Learn something new in an Instant! A short, fast, focused guide delivering immediate results.

2. Use mixins, functions, and variables to dynamically auto-generate styles, based on minimal existing values

3. Use the power of LESS to produce style sheets dynamically, or incorporate precompiled versions into your code

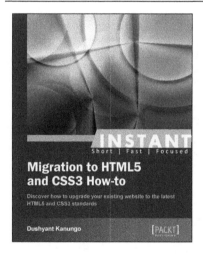

Migration to HTML5
and CSS3 How-to

Instant Migration to HTML5 and CSS3 How-to

ISBN: 978-1-84969-574-9

Discover how to upgrade your existing website to the latest HTML5 and CSS3 standards

1. Learn something new in an Instant! A short, fast, focused guide delivering immediate results.

2. Learn how to upgrade existing websites to HTML5 & CSS3 without changing appearance

3. Improve browser and mobile devices support for websites

Please check **www.PacktPub.com** for information on our titles

www.ingramcontent.com/pod-product-compliance
Lightning Source LLC
Chambersburg PA
CBHW060204060326

40690CB00018B/4247